Better Badminton

Better Badminton

by

Carl H. Jackson

and

Lester A. Swan

Drawings by Evelyn Hawkins

COACHWHIP PUBLICATIONS

Greenville, Ohio

Better Badminton, by Carl H. Jackson and Lester A. Swan
First published 1939.
© 2014 Coachwhip Publications
No claim made on public domain material.
Cover: Shuttlecock © Inge Schepers.

ISBN 1-61646-230-2
ISBN-13 978-1-61646-230-7

CoachwhipBooks.com

To Helen

TABLE OF CONTENTS

TABLE OF CONTENTS (Continued)

TABLE OF CONTENTS (*Continued*)

Introduction

Badminton in this country presents an interesting case of "arrested development." The game is of course a direct lineal descendant of battledore and shuttlecock. Its origin is therefore traceable to India, but its name comes from England—from Badminton, country seat of the Duke of Beaufort. The actual connection between Badminton and the game as played today, or its importance in the history of the sport, is not clear. The name, in any event, has stuck. The game was introduced into New York in 1878 by two gentlemen, one returning from India and the other from England.* In spite of the fact that the club founded by them has remained in existence ever since (it is the oldest badminton club in the world with a continued existence), the game remained relatively obscure in this country until its renaissance in recent years. Since this revival of interest, its growth has been rapid, until today it is one of the fastest, if not *the* fastest growing sport in this country.

The first real impetus on this side of the Atlantic came with the return of the soldiers from the World War. Many officers, Canadian and American, became acquainted with the game in England, where it was already well established. Naturally this was more especially true of the Canadians, which is one reason why the game took hold earlier and has reached a higher state of development in Canada. The founding of a national association is a fairly good indication of the state of development. The Canadian Badminton Association was founded in 1921, while the American Badminton Association came into being in 1936.

More recently, the depression added further stimulus. Seeking new outlets for enforced leisure, which would at the same time not entail great expense, many turned to badminton. For this they found the school gyms well suited. We find in Canada, however, that the churches have provided much of the playing space, many of them being in possession of halls or buildings suited to the purpose; in fact, more players have been accommodated over there through the churches than through the clubs proper. Unlike here, the schools have played little or no part. Perhaps we shall yet find in this country a greater use made of halls (or other suitable buildings) for badminton than at present.

In some respects, badminton is unique as a sport. It has speed, demand on physical reserve and competitive appeal, but its wide adaptability makes

---

An interesting account of the beginnings of the Badminton Club of the City of New York, by Walter Rysam Jones, appeared under the title of "Patriarch of Badminton," in "Canadian Lawn Tennis and Badminton"—December, 1937.

it well suited to all degrees of skill, to all ages and to both sexes. It is an ideal co-recreational sport which boys and girls, men and women, may play with and against each other, since the differences of speed and skill are not so apparent as in most other sports. It is practically the only sport (narrowly defined) which is suited to the purpose indoors. Indeed, the Recreation Training Institute, if we may take press reports* literally, has gone so far as to recommend badminton as a means of keeping marriages from "going on the rocks." At any rate, it is an excellent substitute for many less desirable forms of "co-recreation."

That it is played and enjoyed over a long span of years, by the not-so-young as well as the young, may be easily demonstrated. This is even true of competitive badminton. In looking over the long roster of English badminton champions from 1900 on*, one is struck by the frequent alternate appearance of the same individual over a span of years. Mrs. R. C. Tragett, for example, won the All England Women's Singles Championship in 1912 and duplicated the feat in 1928—a span of sixteen years. Further than that, she won her first doubles championship in 1908 and won the title again in 1926.**

The explanation for this wide adaptability of badminton is found in the nature of the shuttle (or bird). The construction of the bird imparts certain peculiarities to its flight which make the game primarily one of strategy (or "head work") rather than of physique. There is, however, ample opportunity for the use of strength (indeed it is practically a necessity) for a good "smash" and "clear" shot. Hit hard, the shuttle travels at a terrific pace but—its speed is quickly spent. Thus, given equal stroking abilities, the winning of a game is dependent largely on the opponents out-smarting one another by placement and deceptive tactics. Possessing inferior stroking ability, on the other hand, the "smart" player may well overcome the handicap. Herein lies an essential difference between badminton and tennis.

While badminton is played mostly indoors, it can be and is played out of doors. The original game as played in India was an outdoor game. In the southern parts of California, where the wind dies down consistently in the

---

**Reported in "The Detroit Times" (INS)—May 24, 1938.*

** See: "Spalding's Official North American Badminton Guide" (for the Season 1937-38) Edited by Robert D. Forster (Canadian Sports Publishing Company, Brantford, Ontario—1937).

** See page 62—"Badminton for Beginners," by Mrs. R. C. Tragett (Chatto & Windus, London—1935).

late afternoon, the game is played mostly out of doors and is growing rapidly in favor. In fact, we are told on good authority (not by the press agent) that the game is popular with the film colony, and that many of its members play it in their yards. Even in Northern climes the game can be played almost any summer's day, early in the morning or evening, and it has become quite generally a part of the summer camp program. In most camps the space and a spot sheltered from the wind may be conveniently found. The fact that the racket* is light enough to be easily wielded by small children is also a factor in the popularity of the game at boys' and girls' camps.

From the facts cited above, it is evident that badminton is an ideal "carry-over" sport—one which may be played and enjoyed in and out of school, and in the years to come. From these and certain other features, such as safety and economy of space, it follows that the sport fits well into the school or college physical education program. It is rapidly becoming an important part of that program where this is not already the case.

*   *   *

The advent of badminton as a popular sport, and the lack of material sufficiently simplified and illustrated for the beginner, are in our opinion ample justification for this book. The material is the result of several years of playing acquaintance with the game and more than five years of teaching experience. This teaching experience has been with varied groups—children, young people, and adults—mostly under school auspices. Added to this, we have had the invaluable guidance of an expert and veteran of competitive badminton, Mr. Rees Cramer, of Detroit.

As is evident from a hasty perusal of the book, we have relied largely on a visual presentation, attempting to keep the words to a minimum. It is our belief that a volume written for the beginner, for his use when he is starting the game and needs guidance most, is of little value to him unless approached from this angle. When you say for instance that a certain position is best suited for service from the right court (in order to effect a deceptive placement) because of the angle at which the server stands in relation to the receiver's court, the fact is quickly made evident with the use of an appropriate diagram. To the experienced player, the words themselves are sufficient, but for the beginner whose experience is very limited, the diagram saves him much

---

*For the benefit of any who may question the spelling of "racket," we refer you to Webster's or an entertaining discussion of the case of "racket" vs. "racquet" in "American Lawn Tennis and its Badminton Section"—Nov. 20, 1936.

needless pondering, or loss of the point entirely. This is not a reflection on the beginner's understanding. He can't be expected to visualize situations which are unfamiliar to him.

The book is organized in progressive teaching or learning steps, which we believe will prove of value to the coach and instructor in organizing his teaching procedure. It is not expected that the beginner will read through from beginning to end with a view to carrying out suggested techniques before he acquires the necessary experience. It is expected that he will attempt to apply these suggestions in their order as he progresses. The first six chapters will give him sufficient background and techniques to occupy him during his period of "growing pains," which, incidentally, the badminton convert will find is of less duration and much less "painful" than in most sports.

*   *   *

Most of the contents of this book have appeared in the same or somewhat varied form in the following magazines: SCHOLASTIC COACH (April, May, June, 1938), JOURNAL OF HEALTH AND PHYSICAL EDUCATION (March, 1938), JOURNAL OF PHYSICAL EDUCATION —Y.M.C.A. (July-August, 1938), THE SPORTING GOODS DEALER (August, 1938), CANADIAN LAWN TENNIS AND BADMINTON (Several issues, commencing with October 1938).

To their editors, Owen Reed, Elmer D. Mitchell, H. T. Friermood, H. G. Heitzberg, and Robert D. Forster, we wish to extend our thanks for permission to use the material in this book.

We also wish to thank Mr. F. S. DeGalan, Director of Evening Schools, Detroit, and Messrs. Powells, Brown and Collins of Northern Evening School, Detroit, for their cooperation.

Further, thanks are due Mr. C. C. Petersen of Toronto, Ontario Representative of CANADIAN LAWN TENNIS AND BADMINTON, for his encouragement.

To Mr. Norman R. Williams of Detroit we owe thanks for setting this project in motion and materially assisting in the early planning of the work.

Most of all, we are indebted to Mr. Rees Cramer of Detroit for his forbearance and patient criticism. While he shares credit for the book's merits, we assume full responsibility for its faults.

C. H. J.
L. A. S.

CHAPTER I

The Grip and Flexible Wrist

The first step toward BETTER BADMINTON is to acquire the proper racket grip. The effectiveness of badminton strokes (excepting the lift stroke at the net) is dependent on the flexibility of the wrist. Flexibility and power are only possible when the racket is held properly.

Position of the Fingers

To acquire this all-important and fundamental grip, first lay the racket handle in the palm of the hand with the flat face of the racket parallel to the floor. Now hold the racket by firmly wrapping the little finger around the extreme end of the handle, permitting the racket head to point downward. (Fig. 1a)* Now concentrate on the positions of the index finger and thumb, both of which are very important in that they direct every stroking movement.

Curve the index finger around and underneath the facets or sides of the handle and place the thumb well forward on the top of the side-facet, that is, over the circle shown on the handle in Figure 1a. The two remaining fingers will naturally spread apart and around the handle to prevent the racket from slipping or turning. (Fig. 1b) These two fingers together with the little finger may be termed the "anchor fingers."

Position of the Thumb

Now turn the racket from an open-face (face up) to a vertical position, that is, to a position in which the stringed area is at right angles to the floor. If the anchor fingers remain in the position indicated above, it will be observed that the index finger and thumb form a large V or open wedge. (Fig. 1c) With the open wedge well formed and the stringed area or face at right angles to the floor, raise the arm and racket into playing position. (Fig. 1d) The grip should not be tight but merely firmed at the instant of the bird-racket contact and relaxed again immediately after contact.

Wrist Position and Flexibility

The grip, or position of the fingers on the racket handle, is not the only factor to be considered in getting maximum flexibility and power in the wrist

---

*It is assumed throughout these pages that the player is right-handed.

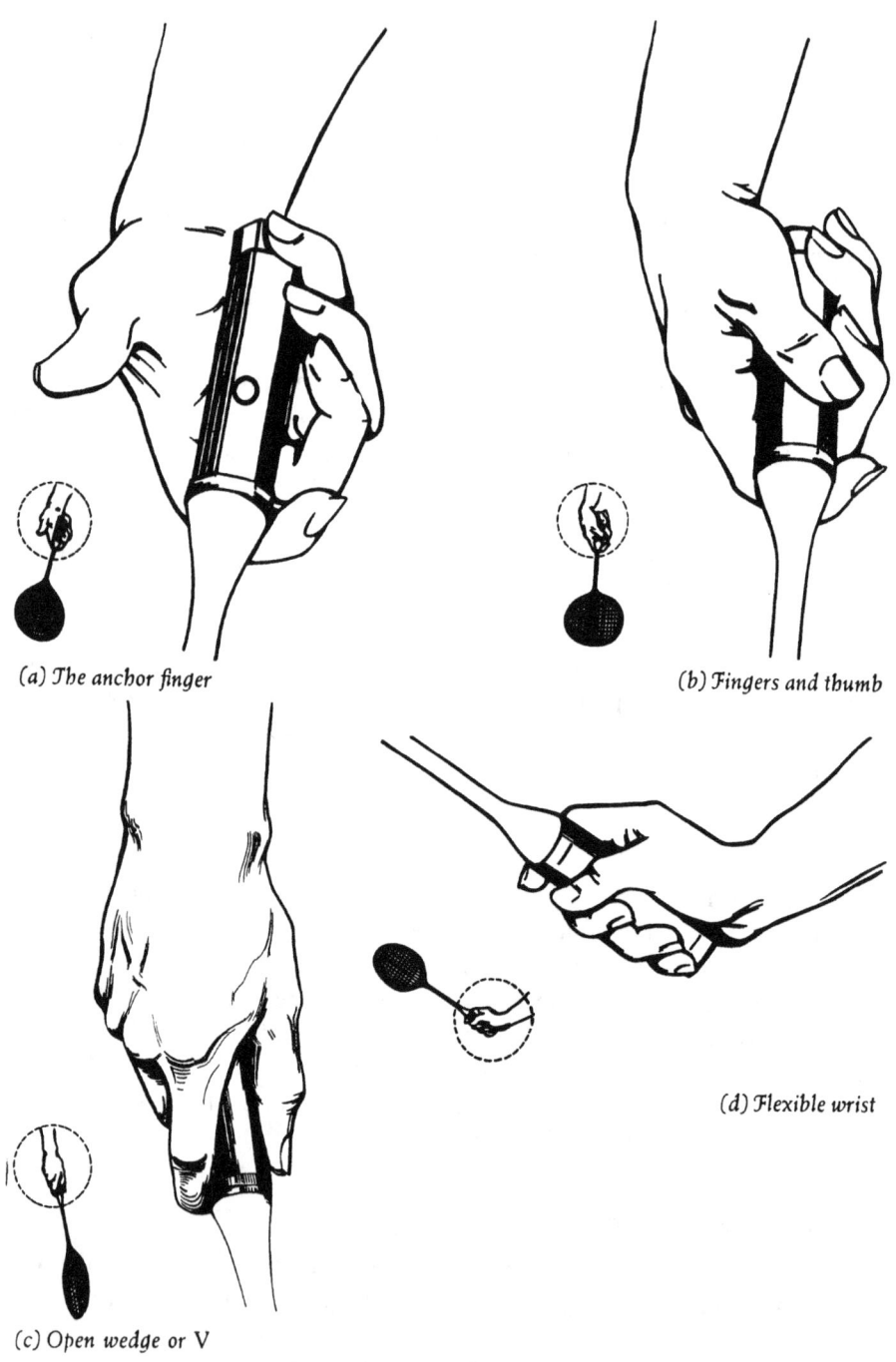

(a) The anchor finger

(b) Fingers and thumb

(d) Flexible wrist

(c) Open wedge or V

Fig. 1: The Grip and Flexible Wrist

16

movement. Equally important is the position of the wrist itself in relation to the arm and racket-head.

Unlocking the Wrist

The wrist is so constructed that when the hand and racket are held in a certain position, the wrist tends to lock or restrict itself in movement. To illustrate, hold the racket with the grip described above, but with the hand bent slightly downward so that the handle of the racket is parallel with the forearm while the elbow, wrist, and tip of the racket are in line with one another. (See "Common Grip Faults," Number 4, below.) Now try to swing the racket back and forth from the wrist, moving only the racket and hand, with the wrist acting as a hinge. It will be noted that the movement is definitely restricted. Attempting to stroke the bird with this "locked" or inflexible wrist limits the direction and flexibility of movement.

Now, from the position described above, tilt the racket slightly upward so that the wrist is slightly lower than an imaginary line between the elbow and the tip of the racket. This position of the wrist may be easily acquired by lowering the wrist slightly, or by tipping the head of the racket slightly upward, or both. (See Fig. 1d) It will be noted that this wrist position gives the maximum freedom of movement. The beginner is urged to give careful study to Figure 1d. The flexible wrist position as described relates to the return and toss service strokes and not entirely to the service stroke which will be described in the next chapter. Recently enacted rules require that the tip of the racket be lower than the wrist at the moment of bird-racket contact in the service. This is a recognition of the fact that the flexible wrist position gives more advantage to the server than is consistent with the spirit of the rules. Therefore, in the simplest service (the out-of-hand) full wrist flexibility will not be possible; but this will not alter the effectiveness of that type of service, where a powerful stroke is to be avoided.

Flexibility for the "Wrist-Snap" and "Flick"

The importance of acquiring the flexible-wrist position along with the correct finger positions cannot be stressed too strongly. Without correct grip and adequate wrist-flexibility, the beginner can never hope to advance to the stage of even a mediocre player. As we shall see later, this wrist action is of the greatest importance in learning the "wrist-snap" and "flick." The reader will readily understand the significance of this statement if he visualizes the "flick" as an arm and wrist movement similar to that used by the whip-artist. We shall return to this subject in a later section.

Practice Hints for Attaining Wrist Power

Once the player acquires the correct grip and learns to keep it, wrist power and flexibility may be increased by practice in driving old birds against the wall and stroking them on the rebound, using both the forehand and backhand strokes.* This may, of course, be practiced outside the gymnasium. The type of practice suggested here is especially recommended to develop the powerful backhand and forehand returns so essential in strenuous competition. Even the champion finds it necessary to constantly check the correctness of his racket-grip and to practice in order to retain and develop flexibility and power in his "wrist-snap" and "flick." It was the strength and flexibility of Walter Kramer's wrist action and his strategic (and deceptive) use of this that made him U. S. amateur champion of 1937 and 1938.

Common Grip Faults**

Rapid development in the game depends on an early recognition and correction of faults. It is fortunate for the badminton player that most of the faults in any department of the game can be grouped into a few types, thus making easy their recognition and suggestion for correction. A summary of faults is perhaps as important as the description of an ideal pattern, since any imitation of the ideal is likely to take on some of the misunderstandings and inaccuracies of individuality. Needless to say, these inaccuracies will be harder to correct the longer they remain unrecognized.

1. Thumb on top (Fig. 2a)—The thumb is on the top facet of the handle instead of on the side facet (i.e., the circle). As a result, the fingers are out of position also. This grip is insecure, especially for the backhand strokes.

2. Index finger fault (Fig. 2b)—The index finger is too far forward on the handle. This grip restricts the movement of the wrist.

3. Combination of faults (Figs. 2c and 2d)—In Figure 2c, the racket is faced to the player, i.e., when the handle is parallel with the floor, the face is parallel rather than at right angles to the floor; the grip is too tight, the thumb and index finger are out of position. In Figure 2d, the racket is faced properly but cocked up too high, and the grip is too tight.

4. Humped or locked wrist (Fig. 2e)—There is no tilt to the racket here. The

---

*J. F. Devlin relates that he discovered for himself the wrist action by just this practice, at the age of 12. See p. xiii—"Badminton for All" (Doubleday Doran—1937).
**In reference to the common "faults" of players we have in mind the usual meaning of the word, and not "faults" as understood in the Rules.

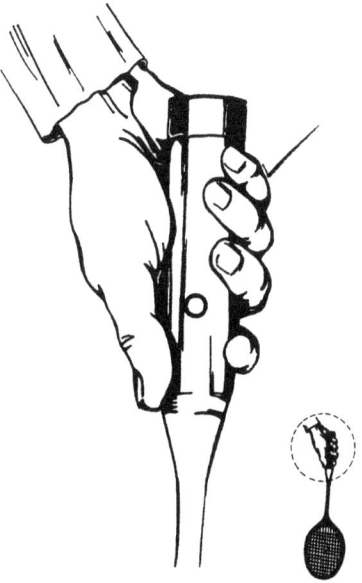

(a) Thumb on top

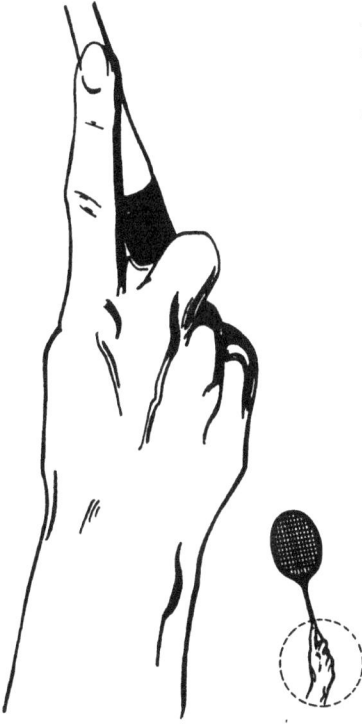

(b) Index finger fault

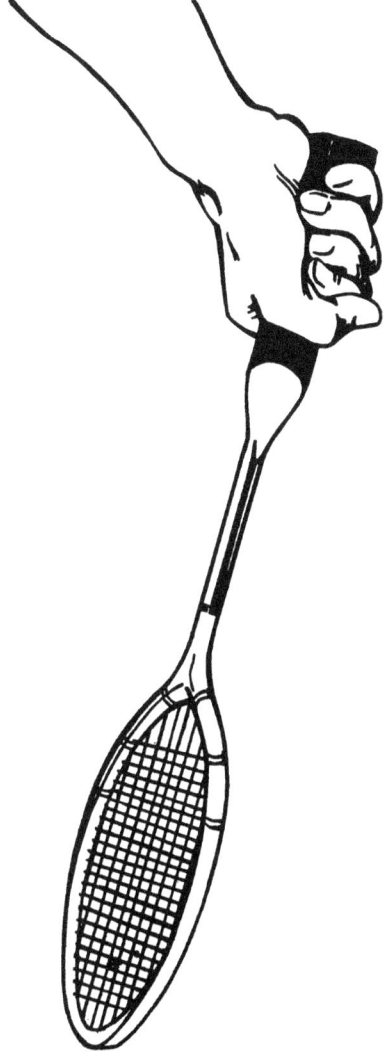

(c) Combination of faults

Fig. 2: Grip Faults

(d) Combination of faults

(e) Humped or locked wrist

(f) Choked grip

Fig. 2: *Grip Faults* (cont.)

handle is on a line with the forearm. (Compare with Fig. 1d) Beginners commonly raise the arm at the elbow, in adjusting the racket for contact with the bird, leaving the wrist locked as shown here.

5. Choked grip (Fig. 2f)—This also illustrates a combination of faults. The racket is faced wrong, the thumb and index finger are out of position and the fingers are crowded. Further, the grip is too tight and too far up the handle. As will be evident later, it would be impossible to get a powerful "smash" using this grip.

CHAPTER II

The Service Made Easy

By service, of course, is meant the act of placing the bird into play at the start of a regular game. The service treated in this chapter is what we may call the out-of-hand, to distinguish it from the more difficult but commonly used toss service. The toss is not recommended for the beginner because of the added complication of timing; for that reason it will not be treated until later in this book, on the assumption that the player will then be better coordinated for badminton. The beginner will find the out-of-hand serve more accurate. The toss should be reserved until he becomes proficient enough to use it without the danger of "popping up" to the receiver and getting a "smash" in return.

The out-of-hand serve offers a quick way for the beginner to prepare himself for doubles play in a group more advanced than himself. The average person may achieve more accuracy in fifteen minutes or so of practice with this type of service than he would in hours spent on the toss service.

While this serve is in common use, in some instances by advanced players, we do not recommend it as a substitute for the toss serve. On the contrary, we recommend a change to the toss serve as soon as the player is sufficiently coordinated for it. If he comes to the game with sufficient aptitude he would do well to start with a toss serve.

Serving Stance

For the serving stance, face the side-lines of the court with the left side of the body toward the net. With the racket and bird held out in front, ready for service, extend the right foot backward. (Fig. 3) The weight should be on the forward (left) foot. This left-foot-forward stance is the more natural for this type of forehand stroke and hence easier for the beginner. As control and accuracy are acquired, however, the player may prefer to change, for defensive reasons, to the right-foot-forward stance. Of this we shall have more to say later.

Holding the Bird

Hold the bird lightly by the extreme tip of one of the feathers, that is, between the index finger and thumb, as if pinching salt. Permit it to hang down

Fig. 3: *Serving Stance*

Fig. 4: *Holding the Bird—Out-of-hand Serve*

naturally, that is, perpendicular to the floor. (See Fig. 4) Care should be taken not to extend the ends of the fingers more than a quarter of an inch down the shaft of the feather, to prevent the frame of the racket from hitting the fingers when the bird is struck. If this precaution is heeded, there need be no fear of hitting the fingers. Note in Figure 3 that the bird is held fairly well out in front of the body to prevent a cramping of the racket-swing. It should be observed further that the bird is struck on its side. The construction of the bird and its characteristic flight do not require that it be pointed into the face of the racket as some beginners suppose.

The rules for service require that the bird be *not* hit *above* the *waist* line or the *hand holding* the *racket*. It will be necessary, therefore, to adjust the bird, arm and racket accordingly, as shown in Fig. 5.

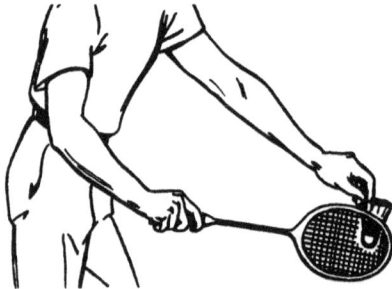

(1)

(4)

(2)

(5)

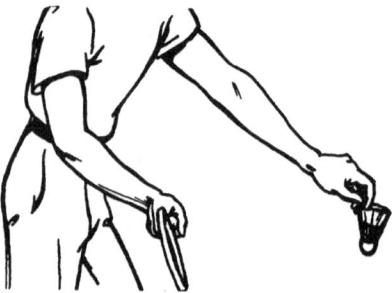

(3)

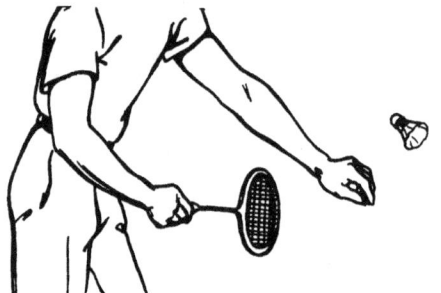

(6)

Fig. 5 : *Out-of-hand Service Stroke*

The Out-of-Hand Service Stroke

As cautioned a moment ago, hold the racket and bird fairly well away from the body. This is the position best suited to the wrist action of the out-of-hand service. Now focus the eye on the bird and adjust the latter to the racket tip (not the racket to the bird) as shown in Figure (3) and (5); then take a few practice swings to make sure that the racket and bird are in proper alignment for accurate contact *on the strings* (not the frame). The bird should be adjusted *to* the racket-swing and a few trial swings taken to effect perfect alignment.* The popping sound resulting from contact of wood and bird is indicative of a faulty alignment between bird-cork and racket-frame. In this, of course, the bird is not hit close enough to the fingers.

The backswing and the stroking movement are from the wrist entirely. It is as though the racket were a gate swinging on its hinge, the wrist. This is clearly demonstrated in the photo-sequence of Figure 5. Note that the arm holding the bird has not moved out of position; the same is true of the bird until it is hit, indicating that *it has actually been struck out of the hand* and has *not* been *dropped* or *tossed*.

In tapping the bird, approach it cautiously and then "flick" it suddenly, as if hitting at a fly with a swatter. (The "flick" in this type of stroke is not, of course, the same sweeping, whiplike racket movement used in the return strokes.) Further, the bird is tapped *lightly* since the object is to so gauge the stroke that the bird falls just over the short service line. (See Fig. 7 for court lines) Care should be taken to keep the bird flight very close to the net tape.

Court Position

The beginner should practice the service in the court position most commonly used. In the singles game, the position for serving in each court is similar, that is, near the midcourt line and about four feet back of the short service line. (See Fig. 7 for court lines) This position is selected for defensive reasons, being approximately equidistant from the farthest corners. In the doubles game, the service position should be closer to the alley and about a racket's length back of the short service line. Other (and more precise) service positions will be explained later. For the present, the beginner is advised to devote most of his time to becoming proficient in delivering a service close to the net and just over the short service line—preferably to the corners of the receiving court.

Many players serve poorly because they lack a clear picture of the steps and have not formed the habit of taking the time to think them through. This thinking-through or check-up of all points for accurate preparedness makes for a precise service, and, of course, BETTER BADMINTON.

Summary of Steps in the Service

1. Check the GRIP as outlined in Chapter I.
2. Assume serving STANCE (a racket's length back of the short service line for doubles and four feet back for singles), feet and body facing the side-

---

The "practice swings" are suggested here for practice only and should not be used in actual play since they constitute a feint as defined in the Laws. (See Law 14 (d) and Interpretation 1 appended to the Laws.)

lines, left foot forward, weight forward on the left foot, right foot back to act as balance and anchor for pivoting.

3. HOLD the bird by the TIP of a feather between the index finger and thumb, and fairly well OUT IN FRONT of the center-line of the body. Allow the bird to hang down perpendicularly, so that it may be struck on its side.

4. Look at the net tape and locate the height. Look at the bird, retaining in your mind a visual memory of the height of the net. Keep your eye on the bird.

5. ADJUST the bird to the racket, keeping both fairly well out in front of the body and SWING the end of the racket back and forth from the wrist-hinge, without moving the arm.

6. "FLICK" the bird softly out of the fingers.

Faults in the Out-of-Hand Serve

1. Moving the whole arm—This is a sort of "push" stroke—a very common fault of beginners in all strokes. In the service, this is again a failure to use the "gate swing."

2. Legs stiff, feet flat—Failure to relax and assume a position for quick movement. In short, the player is not "on his toes."

3. Directional fault of flight—There are two main reasons for this fault: the hips may be pointed incorrectly (not in line with the proposed flight); or the racket may not be at right angles to the proposed line of flight at the moment of contact.

4. Fault in angle of flight—That is, in upward angle of flight. As already noted, flights at a sharp upward angle leave the server open for a "smash" return. This fault may result from: the racket itself being lofted, i.e., not at right angles to the floor; or stroking with a circular underswing instead of the "gate swing."

5. Extending the finger down feather shaft (Fig. 6b)—When held this way, the bird is of course either dropped or tossed, inaccurately; or the fingers are hit and injured. Fear of hitting fingers may result also, with a consequent pulling in of the service stroke.

6. Extending thumb down feather shaft (Fig. 6c)—Another tendency of the beginner, in the out-of-hand serve. Note dotted line indicating the racket.

A Note on Service Rules

In using this serve, care should be taken to keep the bird *below the waist* and the *head of the racket below the hand holding the racket.* (See Law 14 (a)) One is apt to raise the bird and head of the racket to an illegal position without realizing it.

Objection has been raised in some quarters to a "preliminary flourish" of the racket as employed by some players who use this serve. Such a flourish is unnecessary and is probably done without the player being conscious of it. We have suggested measuring bird and racket, as shown in Figure 5 (1), and then making a single backswing, as shown in Figure 5 (1) through 5 (3). This can be done with one continuous motion and without any perceptible or misleading hesitation. It does not seem to us that this can be construed as a feint within the meaning of Law 14 (d) and Interpretation 1 appended to the Laws. Even this backswing, however, may be dispensed with if one wishes. The stroke may be started from the position shown in Figure 5 (3) or no further back than shown in Figure 5 (2).

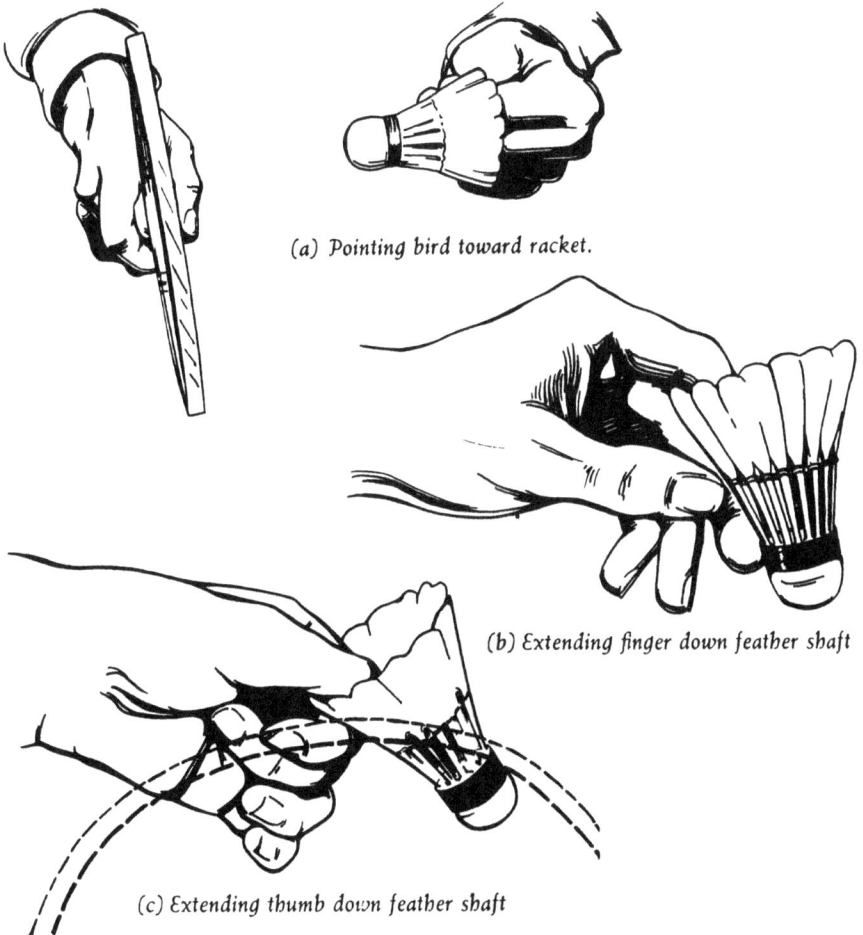

(a) Pointing bird toward racket.

(b) Extending finger down feather shaft

(c) Extending thumb down feather shaft

Fig. 6: Faults in Out-of-hand Serve

27

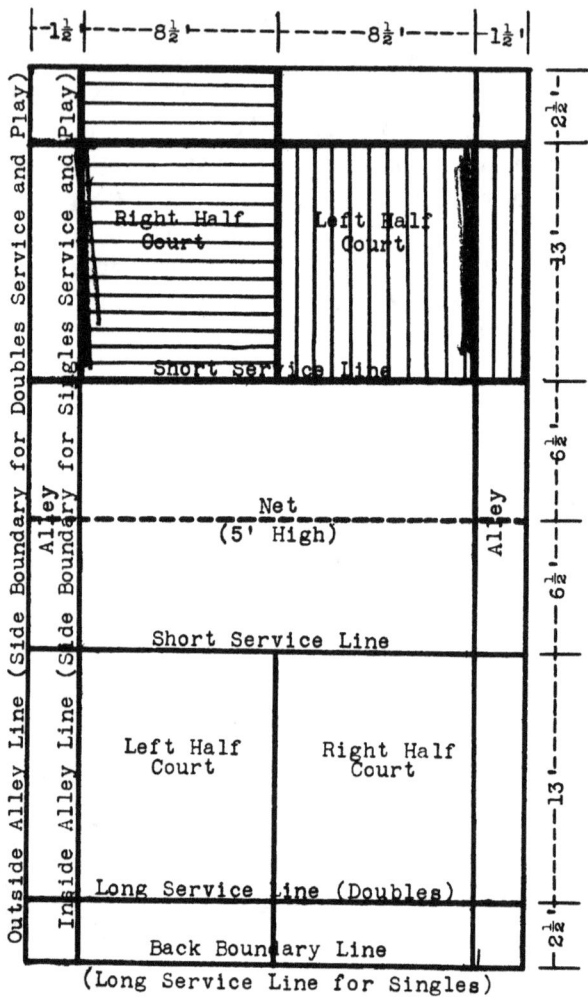

Fig. 7: Court Diagram,

showing lines, dimensions, service and receiving courts

CHAPTER III

Rules and Scoring Simplified—Singles

If conditions permit, it is desirable for the beginner to start with the singles game, though, of course, there is no particular reason why he should avoid doubles at the outset. For clarity, we shall begin with the singles game.

Starting the Game

For choice of side and starting serve, it is customary to spin a racket and guess whether the smooth or rough side of the trim* turns up.

Play at the start of a game always begins with the serve from the right half-court, to the receiver who stands diagonally across the net in *his* right half-court. Only the server scores points, and he continues to serve so long as he continues to win points. One exception to this rule should be noted here. When the bird hits the net tape, as it is served, but falls into the proper court (or is hit by the receiver before falling), a "let" is declared and the service is taken over in the same court, with no point scored. If the server otherwise fails to score, the serve passes to his opponent, and neither scores.

The loss of a serve is termed a "down," or in the language of the English player, a "hand out." Thus, in singles, one "down" or "hand out" concludes the server's inning, whereupon the serve passes to his opponent. In *his* first serve, the opponent likewise serves from the right half-court. The player who is serving is said to be "in service," while the receiver is said to be "out of service," or simply, "in" and "out." During service, both server and receiver must remain within the boundaries of their respective half-courts. (See Fig. 7)** Overstepping, standing on, or touching the boundary line constitutes a "fault," that is, it results in the loss of service or in a point for the opponent. The moment the bird is hit, the server and receiver may move out of the prescribed boundary of the serving and receiving courts.

Scoring and Choice of Service Courts

After the first service, and within the same inning (that is, before one "down"), service alternates from right to left half-court, and from left to right, as each point is won. If the score is kept in mind, the proper court in a singles

---

*The trim is the string at both ends of the racket face and is looped over the lengthwise strings. The side showing the loops is termed the "rough" side.

**In addition, some part of both feet must remain on the floor or ground and in a stationary position. See Rule 16.

match may be determined by a simple rule or memory device. Each point counts 1 (or an "ace"), which means that if the server has a score of 0 or an even number (0, 2, 4, 6, etc.), he should be serving in the right half-court; if he has an odd score (1, 3, 5, 7, etc.), he should be serving in the left half-court. Likewise, knowing the service court, the score may be checked for accuracy.

After the first inning, the server in the singles game always begins his inning by serving from the court where he last served (and failed to score). This court is, of course, more easily determined by applying the rule given above. It is customary to announce the server's score first, after he has taken up his position for the serve. Thus, 1—0 means that the score is 1 to 0 in favor of the player then about to serve; it also means that he should be serving from his left half-court.

The importance of remembering the score is thus apparent. It prevents much confusion. As we said a moment ago, the score should be announced immediately before the serve is made. At that moment, both players will have recovered from the preceding volley, will have taken their places for the next play, and will have had the opportunity of determining in their own minds what the score is. When the proper court is definitely known, this fact, of course, may serve as a check of the score. However, when beginning a new inning, the player has probably forgotten where he served last, and the score is essential to the choice of the proper court. A sample game, to illustrate scoring, choice of courts, and some simple rules will probably help to clarify these matters and fix them in the reader's mind.

Sample Game of Singles

A and B are playing a singles game, and A starts with the serve in his right half-court, B receiving in *his* right half-court. A's first serve is good, a volley ensues, and B drives the bird out of bounds. The score is announced as 1—0, as player A begins service in his left half-court, to player B who now stands in *his* left half-court. On the serve, the bird touches the net tape but falls within B's left half-court. It is a "let,"* no score is made, and A serves over again from the same half-court. This time, A serves into the net; neither A nor B score, but the serve passes to B. A is now said to be "out" and B "in."

The score is announced as 0—1 and B serves, from his right half-court, to A who is standing in *his* right half-court. The serve is good, a volley ensues, until A misses the bird (as it falls within the singles playing boundaries). The

---

In using loose terminology, this is sometimes erroneously called a "net." There is no such term in strict badminton terminology.

score is 1—1 and B serves again, this time from his left half-court. It is a good serve, and after a volley, A drives the bird into the net. The score is now 2—1 as B serves from his right half-court. On this serve, the bird falls short of the receiving court, that is, between the net and the short service line. B is "out" and the service passes to A again, who has forgotten the score and also the court from which he is to begin the inning.

As B takes up his position in his left half-court, A "inquires the call" (asks for the score). B announces the score as 1—2, whereupon A takes up his position for the serve in his *left* half-court. (The server's score is odd, hence he serves from the left half-court. Reference above indicates that this is the court from which he last served but failed to score in his preceding inning.) After a good serve by A, B makes a deft net shot in which the bird hits the net tape but "dribbles" down on A's side of the net and falls dead within the boundary. A is "out" and B is "in."

A announces that the score is 2—1 as B selects his court position for the serve, in the *right* half-court. (When the server's score is 0, 2, 4, etc., or an even number, he begins serving from the right half-court. This, of course, proves to be the court from which B last served in his preceding inning.) In his service attempt, B now misses the bird entirely (not even ticking it). This is not a "fault," that is, it is not considered a failure or "down." B makes the serve over. This time, the bird passes over the net, very close to the net tape, and A thinks it is going to fall "out of court," so he makes no attempt to return it. Instead of going out, the bird falls *on* the midcourt line, near the intersection of the short service line. This is a point for B, and with the score now 3—1, he serves from his left half-court to A, who, of course, stands in *his* left half-court. On this serve, B strikes the bird as he is holding it *above* his waistline. This is a "fault," and B is "out."

The score is announced as 1—3 and A serves from his left half-court. In the exchange of shots which follows, B makes an attempt to return a bird near the outside boundary line—he swings but misses the bird entirely. The bird, however, falls out of bounds. A is nevertheless "down" and the serve goes to B. The score is again 3—1 as B begins service in his *left* half-court.

In the next exchange, B smashes the bird at A, who cannot get completely out of the way or, of course, return it. The bird barely touches his shoulder and falls out of bounds. This is a point for B since the bird touched A. The score is 4—1 and B serves again, this time from his right half-court. In the ensuing volley, A swings at the bird near the boundary line—he barely "ticks" the tip of the bird-feathers with his racket and the bird falls out of bounds. B scores again since A touched the bird.

31

The score is now 5—1 and B serves from his left half-court. In the ensuing exchange, B "rushes" one at the net, and although he returns it, in so doing he touches the net with his racket. Since the bird was still in play as B did this, that is, it was not dead, it is a "fault" and B is "out." (Touching the net with any part of the body, clothing, or racket, while the bird is in play, constitutes a fault.) The serve now passes to A who begins service in his *left* half-court as the score stands 1—5.

For our purposes, we need pursue the play of A and B no further.

"Game"

"Game" points in singles may be established by the customs or rules governing the club or courts; or they may be determined in accordance with local or other conditions, such as the number of persons waiting to play, the limitations on the players' time, etc. In short, this matter is very flexible. The American Badminton Association has established 15 points as "game" for all matches except women's singles. For women's singles, the regulation "game" is 11 points.

In men's singles, "game" may be increased when the score is tied at 2 or 1 less than the prearranged "game," at the option of the player first reaching the tied score. This is called "setting." Thus, in the regular men's singles match, when the score is tied at 13, the player who first reached this score may "set" the game to 5 points. When the score is tied at 14, the player who first reached this score may "set" the game to 3 points.

The game may be "set" in a women's singles match also; in this case, to 3 points when the score is tied at 9 and to 2 points when tied at 10. Here again, the choice of whether or not the game shall be "set" rests with the player first reaching the tied score.

In any case, the choice of "setting" must be made and the number of points decided *before* the service immediately following the tie score is made. In effect, of course, "setting" amounts to increasing the "game," or total number of points, to either 18 or 17 in men's singles and to 12 in women's singles. However, it is customary to call the score "love all" when the game has been "set" and to begin the scoring anew. For example, if the player having the first serve after the game is "set" scores on this serve or the ensuing volley, the score is announced as 1 to 0. The player first reaching the score 5 or 3 (whichever is set) in men's singles wins the game. Similarly, the lady first reaching 3 or 2 (whichever is set) in women's singles wins the game.

"Setting" *tends* to favor the player leading immediately before the score was tied, that is, the player who first reached the tied score and who "set" the game, because his opponent is necessarily serving at that moment. To score, of course, one must be in possession of the serve. "Setting," therefore, tends to increase the chances of the "setting" player to regain the serve. This is not to say that "setting" is an infallible choice, nor that every player elects to "set" the game in the circumstances.

A "rubber" is the best of 3, 5 or 7 games, as may be prescribed. In regulation play it is the best of 3. The opponents change ends at the start of each new game. If it is necessary to play the odd game, they change ends in the last game when the leading score reaches 8 (if it is a 15-point game) or 6 (if it is an 11-point game).

Summary of Elementary Badminton Rules

1. The server and receiver must stand within the boundary of their respective half-courts when the serve is being made.

2. Points are scored by the server only.

3. When the server fails to score (except in the case of a "let"), he loses the serve.

4. The server's score is called first.

5. The first service of a game is from the right half-court. Subsequent services alternate between half-courts, except at the beginning of an inning (*in singles*) when they are made from the right half-court if the server's score is 0 or even, and from the left half-court if the server's score is odd.

6. A *serve* is not legal if the bird is struck at a point above the waistline, or if the head of the racket is above the hand holding the racket.

7. Birds falling on the line are not out of bounds.

8. Serves touching the net and falling within the proper boundaries (or hit by the receiver), should be served over.

9. A server failing to touch the bird during an attempted serve may try again, until the bird has been contacted by the racket or body.

10. If the bird contacts the racket or body while serving, this constitutes a legal serve.

11. If a player misses a bird when attempting to return it, and it falls out of bounds, he wins the point or service, according to which side is "in service." In other words, the result is the same as though he had purposely allowed it to pass.

12. If, during a volley, the bird hits the player or the latter touches the net (with the body, clothing, or racket), either he forfeits the serve or the opponent scores, according to which side is "in service."

13. The bird may not be hit legally until it has crossed the net. The racket, however, may pass over the net in the follow-through, provided the net is not touched while the bird is in play.

14. The bird must be hit *distinctly*, i.e., it may not be "thrown." This is done (accidentally or intentionally) by drawing the racket face away from the bird just before contact, by catching the feathers in the strings, by cutting the bird, or by allowing it to slide off the racket.

15. Legally, the bird may not be hit twice in succession, by a player or his partner, in a single return.

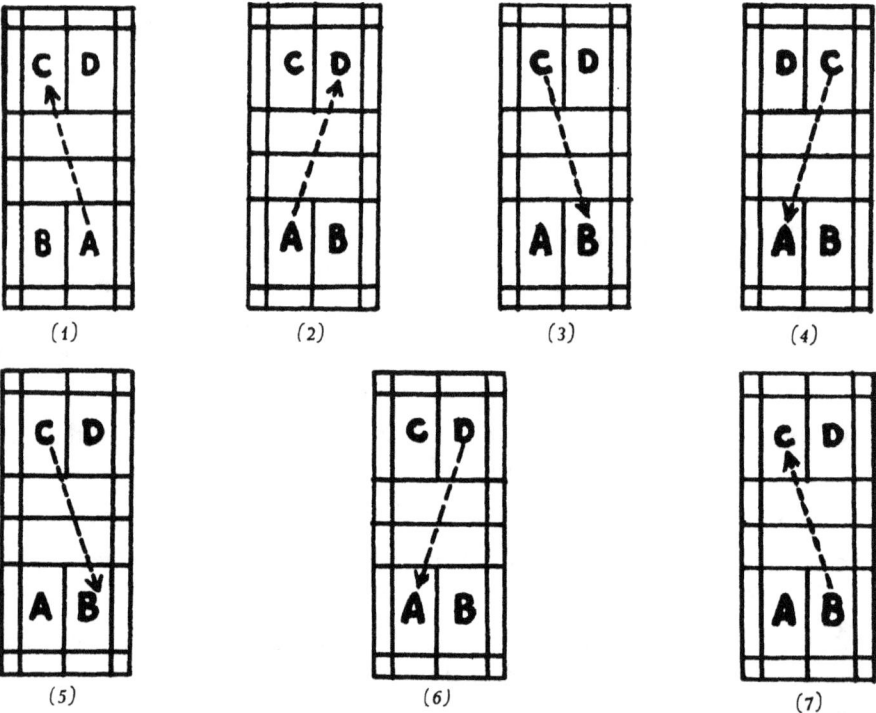

(1) (2) (3) (4)

(5) (6) (7)

(1) A begins service in *right* half-court to C in opposite *right* half-court.
(2) After scoring, A shifts to *left* half-court and serves to D. (Score 1:0)
(3) A and B missed point, serve passes to *other team* and C begins service in *right* half-court to B in opposite *right* half-court. (Score 0:1)
(4) After scoring, C shifts to *left* half-court and serves to A. (Score 1:1)
(5) After scoring again, C shifts to *right* half-court and serves to B. (Score 2:1)
(6) After failing to score, service passes to *partner* D who serves from *left* half-court to A. (Score 2:1)
(7) After failing to score again, service passes over to *other team* and B serves from *right* half-court to C. (Score 1:2)

34   Fig. 8: *Sample Doubles Game*

CHAPTER IV

Rules and Scoring Simplified—Doubles

For most players, the doubles game will be the more frequently played because of the increased fun, sociability, strategy, and finesse of the four-handed game. Essentially, of course, the rules for doubles are the same as for singles. However, there are some differences pertaining to the choice of service courts which, in order to avoid confusion, warrant a separate treatment of the two types of game.

Beginning the Game

As already noted, it is customary at the start of a game to determine the choice of ends and of serving or receiving by means of a spin of the racket. In the games which follow, the side winning the previous game begins service. Play, of course, begins with the serve from the right half-court, to the receiver in the other right half-court, diagonally across the net from the server. Only the side "in service" scores. Points are counted as in singles, one for each gain made by the serving side.

Except in the *first inning* of the game, the serve passes to the partner after the first "down" (or failure to score); on the second down, the serve passes to the other side. Thus each side has two "downs" in any one of its innings, excepting the first inning of the game. In other words, each player on a side has a serve before it passes to the opposing side, with *one* exception—the side having the *first* service of a game has only one "down" in its *first* inning. Thus, as soon as the *first* server's side fails to score, the serve passes to the opposing side, which has *two* "downs" in *its* *first* inning (as in subsequent innings).

In mixed doubles, the lady always begins the game in the right half-court. Thus, she is the first to serve and to receive. Of course, this is a matter of courtesy, not simply from the "ladies-first" standpoint but also because the left court is the more vulnerable, requiring more play from the backhand. Then too, it is from the left half-court that the overhead smash and the severe forehand returns are most frequently made.

Choice of Service Courts

After the first service, and within the *same* inning, the service alternates from one half-court to the other and the server's partner takes up his position in any part of the court so long as he does not interfere with the serve. This applies also to the receiver's partner. The players of the *"out"* side (the receivers) *do not change courts* as the serve alternates. Thus, *receiving* of the serve alternates from one player to the other.

When the server's partner takes up the serve, after the first "down" of the inning, he serves from the alternate half-court, as though the original server had continued to serve. In other words, he serves so that a player of the "out" side does not receive two consecutive serves in any one inning.

The *first serve in each inning* is always from the *right* half-court. This, the reader will note, is contrary to the rule applying in the case of singles. (See page 30) We may, however, use another simple rule or memory device which serves to identify the proper service court in any doubles situation. The rule also serves as a check on the score when the service court is definitely known. The rule is as follows: When a player is serving or receiving the serve in his original court (that is, the court in which he started the game) his side should have either 0 or an even number of points. From this it follows that whenever he is serving or receiving the serve in the *other* half-court, his side should have an odd number of points.

In announcing the score, that of the side "in service" should, of course, be announced first. Scoring and choice of courts are the cause of much confusion to beginners. However, it need not be so, if some effort is made to remember the score and it is applied in the choice of courts. To this end, the score should (as we pointed out in connection with the singles game) *always* be announced as the server is *about* to serve, that is, after the players have recovered from the preceding volley and have taken their places for the next play. This gives time for the player to settle the matter in his mind and permits an adjustment of courts before the play, if necessary.

A sample doubles game will help clarify these matters.

Sample Doubles Game

A and B are playing C and D, and A begins the game by serving from his right half-court, to C, in the other right half-court. (See Fig. 8$^{(1)}$) The serve is good and after an exchange, D drives the bird out of bounds.

The score is 1—0 and is so announced, after A shifts over to the left half-court from where he serves to D. (See Fig. 8$^{(2)}$) Note that C and D retain original half-courts and that B, of course, must shift as A does. In the exchange which follows A's second serve, A drives the bird into the net. The serve passes to the other side.

The score is announced as 0—1, as C begins service to B, who had shifted over to his right half-court for A's last service. (See Fig. 8$^{(3)}$) Note that the A-B team had only one "down" in the *first* inning of the game; also, that C is first to serve for his side because he originally occupied the right half-court, where he remained while his side was "out" (or receiving). C's service is good, a volley ensues, and A finally misses the bird, which falls within the court.

The score is announced as 1—1 after C shifts over to his left half-court; from there he serves to A. (See Fig. 8(4)) A returns the serve, but it is out of bounds.

The score is now 2—1 and C shifts over to the right half-court from where he serves to B, who is still in his right half-court (where he *began* the inning). (See Fig. 8(5)) C serves into the net and is "down."

The score still stands 2—1 as the serve passes to C's partner, D. (Each side gets two "downs," except in the first inning of the game.) D now serves from his *left* half-court, to A. (See Fig. 8(6)) Note that D does not begin *his* service in the right half-court because B would then receive two consecutive serves in an inning. (On the serving side, a change of courts is not permissible except as points are scored. On the receiving side no change is permitted at any time.) After D's serve and a volley, C drives out of bounds, making it two "downs" as the serve passes to the other side.

The score is 1—2 as B begins service. (See Fig. 8(7)) B, of course, begins service in this inning because he is at this time in the *right* half-court, from where service for the inning must begin. It will be noted that the score and service court, as thus determined, meet the test of the rule given above. B started the game in the left half-court; he is *not* serving from the court from which he started the game—thus, his score is and should be an odd number of points.

At this juncture we may leave A, B, C and D to enjoy the remainder of their doubles game.

"Game"

"Game" in doubles, as in singles, is very flexible and may consist of any number of points, as determined at the outset. The regulation doubles game consists of 15 points. These matters may be set to suit time or court limitations. A "rubber" is the same as in singles.

The rules for "setting" in any doubles match are exactly as described for men's singles. (See page 32) The decision of whether or not to "set" a game in a doubles match rests in part on the number of "downs" which the opponents (or serving side) have at the time.

If the serving side has one down already and it is felt that the serve may be regained by "playing out" the remaining two points, it would not, of course, be wise to "set" the game. If the serving side has no "downs," on the other hand, the better choice is probably to "set" the game.

If the side having choice of "setting" the game at a 13—13 tie does not elect to do so, the game may be "set" later if a 14—14 tie occurs. The same applies to singles.

Summary of Badminton Rules (Concluded)

For a full summary of elementary badminton rules see preceding chapter (page 33). These rules will, of course, apply to doubles. We need add only the following:

1. The first service of *any inning in doubles* is from the right half-court.

2. Whenever a player in *doubles* is serving or receiving in the court in which he started the game, his score should be 0 or an even number of points; if not in the original service court, his score should be an odd number of points.

3. In the *doubles* game, the side serving first has only one "down" in its first inning. In all other innings, each side has two "downs."

For complete rules, see Appendix. BETTER BADMINTON necessarily implies a thorough knowledge of the rules. New situations are constantly calling for new applications of the rules, which the reader fails to visualize in the first or even a few readings of them.

CHAPTER V

Bird Flight

Before the strokes are considered, the beginner should first know exactly what he is trying to produce with those strokes. Therefore, we shall consider the subject of bird flight first. Ordinarily, the player thinks in terms of stroking, flights being considered incidental to the stroke only. Stroking and bird flight are, of course, intimately related, in fact, inseparable. But it seems to us that much is to be gained if the two are considered separately, as if distinct. Each flight considered below, of course, involves one or more of the fundamental strokes to be considered in the next chapter.

Introducing Strategy

A consideration of bird flights, moreover, is the simplest approach to the subject of strategy. Badminton depends more on "head work" than on skill and physique, and by the same token, more on bird flight than on the stroking itself. There is, perhaps, no other game of a similar nature where this is quite so much the case. This is one reason why the game is so well adapted to mixed doubles play of men and women. This is why, too, interest in the sport is so frequently kept alive in later years, when the speed and exertion which youth puts into it may give way to a game of "out-foxing" the other fellow. At the same time, a fast singles game calls for the speed and stamina that only the athlete, in the true sense of the word, possesses.

1. *Short Service*

   A very carefully calculated and measured cross-court flight, over the net by a fraction of an inch and directed to a point a trifle inside the short service line, preferably to either corner of the receiving court.

2. *Driven Flight (or Drive)*

   A low, fast flight, parallel or nearly so to the floor, the bird crossing very close to the net tape.

3. *Clear (or Lob)*

   a. High Clear—A long, rapidly ascending flight, high overhead, the bird falling in the backcourt near the baseline.

   b. Driven Clear—Just high enough to prevent opponent reaching the bird and fast enough to beat him to the backcourt.

4. *Smash*

   A very fast, downward flight, at sharp angle to the floor.

5. Drop

A rapidly descending flight, the bird being just over the net by a narrow margin and falling close to the net on the other side.

6. Net Flights

a. Short or "Hairpin" type—Very short and slow, the bird "climbing up" one side of the net, crossing very close to the net tape and "dribbling down" the other side.

b. Cross-court or Driven type—Likewise very close to the net but directed diagonally across the net (along the net tape) and accurately gauged so bird will fall at a point on the court near the net and side alley.

Change of Velocity of Flights

Unlike a ball, the badminton bird, due to its peculiar construction, is subject to a rapid and radical change in velocity and herein lies the secret of the peculiarities of its flight. The energy of the swiftest bird is quickly and suddenly spent in flight, after which it falls abruptly. The change in velocity of flight is, of course, due to (1) the strength with which the bird is hit, (2)

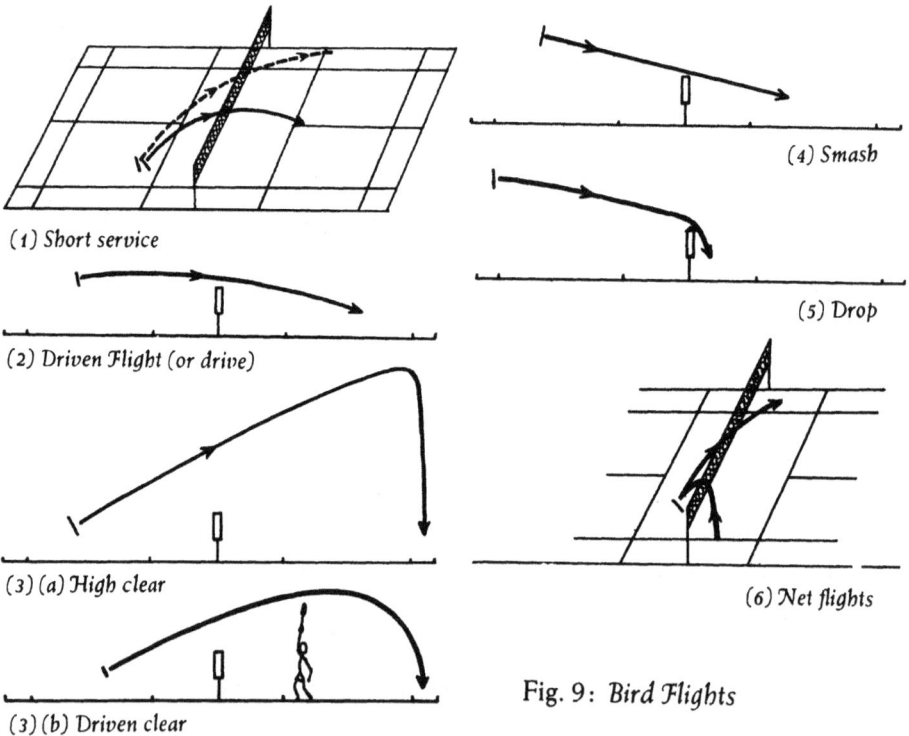

(1) Short service

(2) Driven Flight (or drive)

(3) (a) High clear

(3) (b) Driven clear

(4) Smash

(5) Drop

(6) Net flights

Fig. 9: Bird Flights

the course of flight, that is, the fact of whether it is rising or falling, and (3) the distance through which the velocity is allowed to diminish. On this basis we may classify bird flights into six types as shown in Fig. 9.

Choosing *the* Bird Flight

1. General defensive considerations:
    a. Characteristic flight of oncoming bird (whether a Drive, Smash, etc.).
    b. Position of the receiver (whether out of position or off balance).
2. General offensive considerations:
    a. Placement—
        1. Avoid playing to strength of opponent.
        2. Play for an opening.
        3. Play to unguarded court spot.
        4. Play to opponent's body.
        5. Play to opponent's weaknesses.
    b. Direction—
        1. Direct the bird downward whenever possible—to force the opponent to return upward.
        2. Avoid flights which continue upward after bird crosses the net (excepting the High Clear).
        3. Keep flights close to the net tape (excepting the High Clear and possibly the Smash).
        4. Direct bird cross-court.
    c. Change of speed—"Mix" types of bird flights. (Avoid imitating opponent's bird flight, that is, returning his Drive with a Drive, Clear with a Clear, etc.)

Obviously, the first consideration in any given situation is whether the oncoming bird flight places one on the defensive or not. "Defensive" is a relative term. The more advanced the player becomes, the less he is on the defensive. Thus a situation which proves defensive for the beginner would not necessarily be so for the advanced player. In receiving a well executed Smash, the beginner probably hasn't the time for the niceties of placement and deception. In other words, he is on the defensive and must return the bird as best he can, if at all. Also, he may have been forced out of position and in his haste to re-

41

turn the bird is definitely limited in choice of flight. In such a case, the choice may be no other than a High Clear or simply holding the racket for a rebound.

But aside from the purely defensive situations, the player should constantly strive for placement and deception. If the opponent is especially adept at the Smash, every attempt should be made to keep the bird flight low or out of easy reach. If he is weak in returning the slow net flights, play should be frequently directed to the net areas. The most obvious type of placement is, of course, the unguarded court spot, that is, placing the bird out of easy reach. Directing the flight at the opponent's body is another type of placement.

Playing for the point outright, however, is not always the wise thing to do, particularly if the opponent's skill matches one's own. In this event, one must resort to the strategy of "playing for an opening," that is, maneuvering the opponent out of position or causing him to make a weak return by some other tactic, thus paving the way for the final kill.

Particularly important for the beginner is the matter of direction of flight. By "direction" we mean the upward angle of flight as distinguished from placement. The beginner should avoid "popping" the bird up into the air. Upward flights should be to the backcourt if a set-up for the Smash return is to be avoided. The best Smash defense is to be careful not to "pop up." Direct the flight downward whenever possible. If a Flat or Drive type of flight is used (that is, parallel or nearly so to the floor) keep the bird close to the net tape and out of the middle of the court. If forced to hit up, be sure to Clear all the way to the backcourt and preferably to the corners.

With this brief summary of the general factors involved in the choice of flights, we may now turn to a consideration of each flight separately. We shall attempt to show (1) what situations in general call for each type of bird flight; (2) the advantages derived from each flight in that situation; (3) the main requirements of the flight itself, to be successful.

Of course, the assumption in each case, excepting the High Clear, is that the player is free to make a strategic choice of flight. In this consideration of bird flight we are simply reducing the game to its simplest terms. Many playing factors are necessarily omitted for the sake of presenting a clear and simple picture of the game.

When to Use the Drive

The Drive is used: (1) for quick placement—when the bird may be stroked near the height of and at fairly close range to the net; (2) as a last resort —when the bird must be stroked low from the backcourt.

In the first situation, the Drop *might* be used instead of a Drive, but we are assuming that a quick placement to an unguarded court spot away from the net is the better choice. In the second situation, when the bird must be stroked low from the backcourt, two other flights *could* be used, the Drop and the High Clear. These, however, are very difficult without considerable practice; the bird is too far from the net and too low for the accuracy necessary to make a Drop, and the distance from the opponent's backcourt is too great for the High Clear.

The successful Drive depends mainly on two things: (1) the bird crossing very close to the net tape, (2) gauging the strength of the stroke to prevent (a) continued upward flight of the bird after it crosses the net, (b) driving out of the backcourt bounds.

While the Drive is a fast flight, in contrast to the Drop, it does require some gauging, though not quite as carefully as in the case of the Drop. It is apparent that the Drive of a low bird from the midcourt or farther back, when continuing upward, might otherwise give the opponent a good chance for a kill. With the exception of the High Clear (and Smash, if well placed) the first essential of every flight is nearness to the net tape. Otherwise, the player leaves himself open to the deadliest of all flights, the Smash. Lower flights on the contrary, tend to cause an upward return, thus paving the way *for* a Smash.

When to Use the High Clear

The High Clear is used: (1) when in trouble—that is, you or your partner are out of position and need time for recovery, (2) to take advantage of your opponent's weak court position, (3) when in doubt.

The High Clear does not require the same care in stroking that the other flights do; therefore, it can be made successfully if the player is hurried. Equally important is the fact that it also gives the player more *time* to get in position for the next play. The time interval from the moment the bird is struck until the opponent can strike it in return is of many times longer duration than is the case in any other flight. Forcing an opponent from the net or midcourt to the backcourt uses his reserve energy and reveals any weakness he may have in speed, footwork, stroking, and strategy.

Besides giving time to remedy one's own troubles and hurrying the opponent, the High Clear is effective also from the standpoint of the timing and stroking difficulties which it presents to the opponent. A bird "floating" down from overhead after its momentum is spent (particularly from considerable height) is very difficult to judge. The common fault in this case is to strike too soon (missing the bird entirely) or too late (hitting the bird with the racket down too low).

The success of the High Clear depends on: (1) getting adequate height, thus giving *time* to remedy troubles, (2) getting the necessary length (*all the way* to the backcourt), thus forcing opponent to make a defensive return, or in other words, preventing a kill or severe return, (3) getting the height from which the bird will "float" down of its own weight.

The higher the Clear, of course, the greater the time for recovery. A Clear made from close to the net will ordinarily require greater height than one made from midcourt, in order to allow the same time interval.

For the reasons already given, and because it is a relatively easy return to make, the High Clear is the most frequently used of any single flight (where the player has developed the necessary strength of stroke). It may be used from practically any position on the court, except, possibly, in the backcourt where the player will find that to attain this distance requires much practice. The beginner should note that it is very frequently used close to the net when there is sufficient room between the bird and the net. Of course, here as elsewhere, it is used when caught out of position (necessitating a hurried return and requiring time for recovery of position and balance). The Driven Clear, as the name implies, is a combination of the Drive and Clear—a Clear to get the bird to the backcourt; a Drive for quick placement to an unguarded court spot.

When to Use the Smash

The Smash is used: (1) for the kill—to gain the point outright, (2) when the oncoming bird flight is high—arm plus racket length above the shoulders, as a rule, (3) when the distance from the baseline permits (or in other words, when not too far from the net)—this distance will be *no less* than five feet from the baseline for most players.

The success of the Smash depends on: (1) accurate timing and hard hitting, (2) placement and direction—the most effective of which are: (a) crosscourt, (b) down the alley (sidelines), (c) at the opponent's body, (d) to the baseline.

The Smash is the most effective and severe weapon of offense when combined with strategic placement. The most obvious placement is to the unguarded court areas. Other points of placement are, however, equally effective for different reasons. The most obvious is a placement to the opponent's body.

44

In the case of any fast flight such as a Smash (or Drive), direct the bird as often as possible to the opposite side from where the opponent is carrying his racket at that instant.

Cross-court placement, that is, directing the bird diagonally across the court, is, of course, always more effective if combined with a play to the opponent's weakness (backhand, for instance) or a play to an unguarded court spot. If the opponent is moving in any direction or appears to be set to move in that direction, direct the bird at the court area away from which he is *caught* moving.

Down-the-alley placements are effective since their return is more likely to be outside the court than when the placement is well within the court. Also, this draws the opponent out of position for the next play, thus creating an "opening."

When to Use the Drop

The Drop may be used when the oncoming bird flight is: (1) High—from opponent's High Clear, (2) fast—from opponent's Smash, Drive, or "rush" (quick Smash of player at the net), (3) low—that is, when the bird must be stroked near the floor.

The Drop provides a most effective weapon of offense from the backcourt because a successful Drop allows the opponent little stroking space between the bird and net. This will apply, generally, to higher oncoming flights (particularly the High Clear) for most players. Accurate gauging of stroke for proper distance from the net is rather difficult in the case of the low flights at the backcourt. (See discussion of the Drive above.)

It is apparent, therefore, that the success of the Drop depends on a careful gauging of the stroke so that the bird falls close to the opposite side of the net.

When to Use the Net Flights

Net Flights are used: (1) when the opponent is out of position for a net play, (2) when the bird is falling too close to the net for a High Clear.

The success of the Net Flights depends on: (1) the bird crossing just over the net tape and falling close to the net on the other side, (2) very careful and delicate gauging of the stroke. The net flights require constant practice to keep the requisite stroking touch.

Importance of Bird Flight

The importance of Bird Flight cannot be overemphasized to players at all levels of development. Flight and placement in badminton are much more within the control of the player than in any other game. Hence, successful play depends more on ideal patterns of flight than on conforming to ideal stroking patterns. This is the explanation for the fact that badminton is uniquely a game of "head work" and strategy.

Common Faults in Bird Flight

1. Relying too much on speed of flight and not enough on placement (trying to *smash too much*).
2. "Popping up" (especially in the case of net flights and the serve).
3. Flight too far from the net tape.
4. Returning with the same flight as used by the opponent (e.g., returning a Drive with a Drive).
5. "Overworking" the Drop.
6. Clearing short of the backcourt.

CHAPTER VI

The Four Fundamental Strokes

There are four fundamental types of return strokes in badminton, namely, the forehand, backhand, overhead, and the net strokes. In any playing situation, the first decision to be made is what type of stroke is best suited to the occasion. This is, of course, determined by the direction of the oncoming flight —whether to the right or left side of the body, overhead, or close to the net. This decision will then be followed by a maneuvering into the stroking position or stance for the particular stroke.

I. The Forehand Stroke

The forehand stroke is the most "natural" and hence easiest of the four fundamental return strokes. This is the stroke used when returning the bird from the right side of the body.

Fig. 10: *The Forehand Stance*

The Forehand Stance

When the oncoming bird flight is directed toward the right side of the receiver's body, he pivots to the right and takes his position for a forehand return. The position of the feet in relation to the point of bird-racket contact makes considerable difference in the resulting freedom of stroke action.

First, the pivot to the right is made and the player selects the probable point of bird-racket contact, quickly followed by a decision as to the court spot for the stance. Then the feet, body, and arm are brought into position for the stroke. The feet, at this moment, should be in a position similar to that assumed for the simple service, that is, the player is now facing the side of the court and his body is approximately at right angles to the net. The left foot should be a little in advance of the right, and the body leaning forward. (Fig. 10) At this moment, the player is concentrating on timing, that is, on the decision as to *when* the bird-racket contact is to be made.

The beginner will find it advisable to wait until the bird has fallen to a point below the waistline and far enough away to require an extending of the arm and body to reach the bird. This permits a full racket swing and the wrist action necessary for a powerful stroke. As he becomes more skillful, however, he will gain *strategic* advantage by taking the bird at the highest point possible, sometimes sacrificing stroking ease for strategic gain.

First Attempts with the Forehand Stroke

In his first attempts with the forehand, the beginner should direct the bird flight at the net tape so as to avoid "popping up" into the air. (The "pop-up" is, of course, a perfect set-up for a kill.) A drive or flat type of flight, executed with only moderate strength, and just clearing the net, will be the most successful practice for the beginner.

It is important to remember a fact so obvious that the beginner is apt to overlook it—that is, the court lines and net are stationary, but the players and bird are constantly shifting. The player must retain much of the situation in his memory as he watches the players (before the oncoming bird crosses the net) so as to concentrate on the timing and bird-racket contact when stroking.

Fingering the Grip for the Forehand

More strength and accuracy in the forehand stroke will result from a "fingering" of the grip, that is, moving the index finger slightly forward on the

Fig. 11: *Fingering the Grip for the Forehand*

handle. Also, the thumb may be lowered to prevent binding of the wrist and permit full flexibility. (Fig. 11)* Otherwise, the grip remains precisely as described in Chapter I.

Getting the "feel of the swing" as the end of the racket progresses through the air during the stroke marks the player's departure from the beginner's class. This feeling or nerve sense will grow with practice and in the formation of stroking patterns, until one "automatically" senses the accurate racket angle, the correct amount of strength in the stroke and the proper timing of the swing.

How to Stroke from the Forehand

The path of the racket, in the forehand stroke, describes the letter "C" with a long, flat tail. The completion of the stroke should be with a straight, forward movement of the racket—not upward As cautioned in the discussion of the grip and flexible wrist, the head of the racket should be kept above the wrist.

It is important to get a full backswing and plenty of wrist action into the stroke. The backswing should begin as the left foot is being brought forward and set for the forehand stance. The beginner usually waits too long before starting the backswing with the result that he is forced to make a short "push" stroke. For a full backswing, and to get the shoulder into the stroke, the player's back should be actually turned toward the oncoming bird at the completion of the backswing. In stroking, snap the wrist by keeping it in advance of the head of the racket until a moment before contact.

Summary of Action in the Forehand Stroke

1. It has been decided that the oncoming bird will fly toward some point to the right of the body.

---

*This index finger position is very noticeable in the forehand grip of *Walter Kramer, American Amateur Champion.*

2. Pivot and start in the direction of the bird flight.

3. Select the point of bird-racket contact. The correctness of the stance, timing, and stroke depends to a considerable extent on the accuracy of this decision. Some slight adjustments after this selection and before the stroke is completed may, of course, be made.

4. Select the court spot for the forehand stance, beginning the backswing as you come into position.

5. Assume the forehand stance with the left foot a little ahead of the right, with the body faced toward the sidelines.

6. "Finger" the grip for the forehand stroke, that is, move the index finger forward and thumb down slightly.

7. Focus the eye momentarily on the net tape, retaining its height in visual memory.

8. Focus the eye on the bird and adjust timing and stroking if necessary. Be sure to keep your eyes on the bird.

9. Take your time in the stroke! (But *hurry into position* so that you will have the necessary time.) In practice, permit the bird to reach the front of the body and to fall below the waist before stroking (until you can time the stroke at higher levels).

10. Stroke with a straight, forward movement toward the net tape and keep the racket face at right angles to the floor to avoid "pop-ups." As the arm and racket are brought forward, keep the wrist a little in lead of the head of the racket and snap the wrist a moment before contact.

II. The Backhand Stroke

The backhand stroke is used in returning a bird approaching the left side of the body.

When the player receives the bird on the left side, he of course pivots to the left and starts toward the court spot for the backhand stroke. The action sequence is of course the same as described for the forehand stroke.

The Stance for the Backhand Stroke

The backhand stroke requires a stance with the *right* foot forward as contrasted to the forehand stroke. The right foot is placed in advance of the left foot to permit an easier turning movement or winding up of the body, arm, and shoulder in the backswing. (Fig. 12) This permits a full and free swing

Fig. 12: *The Backhand Stance.*

of the racket. For the backhand stance, it is more important than in the forehand that the player keep well away from the bird and stroke at the full reach of the arm and racket. This full reach and freedom of "swing" is one of the most important requirements of a strong backhand.

Fingering the Grip for the Backhand

The fingering of the grip for the backhand stroke is likewise opposite to that of the forehand. The thumb moves up and the index finger down. (Fig.

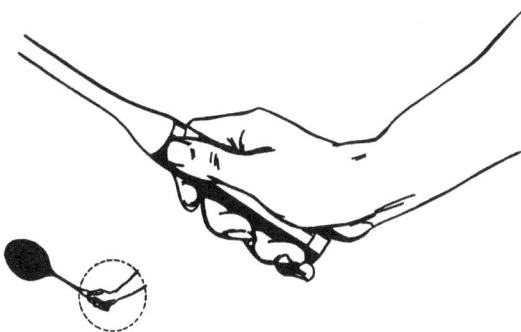

13) The thumb-up position strengthens the leverage on the racket and guides the stroke; the index finger drops down to permit a more flexible wrist action. Other than this, there is no change in the grip.*

Fig. 13: *Fingering the Grip for the Backhand*

*Players who have developed a powerful "wrist-snap" and "flick" do not always use the thumb-up grip. However, it is to be recommended. In any event, it has no disadvantages.

51

How to Stroke from the Backhand

As in the forehand stroke, the path of the racket describes the letter "C" with a long, flat tail. The completion of the swing is not upward, but straight out to make a level forward swing. The head of the racket should be kept above the wrist with the flat face at right angles to the floor.

As the right foot comes forward for the stroking stance, body and arm are wound up in the backswing. The backswing should not be delayed. The body should be turned so that at the end of the backswing the back and shoulders are actually toward the oncoming bird.

The backswing begins with a cocking of the wrist, i.e., the racket is pointed upward from the wrist. At this point the racket is circled over the shoulder and brought downward to a point below the waistline, on a level with the point at which the bird is to be struck. The cocking of the wrist places it in advance of the racket, in which position it should remain until a moment before contact. As the backswing is completed, the wrist, shoulders, spine, hips, and legs are fully wound-up, ready to be released for a strong, backhand stroke. In bringing the racket forward, keep the wrist in advance of the racket-head until a moment before contact, when the wrist should be suddenly snapped. This brings the racket-head forward with much greater force than could be got otherwise.

Summary of Action in the Backhand Stroke

1. It has been decided that the bird will fly toward some point to the left of the body.
2. Pivot to the left and start in the direction of the bird flight.
3. While pivoting, decide on the angle of flight and pace of the oncoming bird, then select the point of bird-racket contact and the court spot for the backhand stance. Remember to keep well away from the bird.
4. Assume the backhand stance, with the right foot forward, toward the sidelines.
5. As the right foot is placed in position for the stroking stance, begin the backswing of the body and racket, cocking the wrist into position as the racket is brought in front of the body.
6. Finger the grip to a thumb-up position as the backswing begins.
7. Note the net tape height, then focus the eye on the bird, and adjust the timing.
8. Keep the wrist leading the racket until an instant before the bird-racket contact.

9. Complete the stroke with a "snapping" movement of the wrist.

10. Practice for power in your stroke.

III. The Overhead Stroke

In the overhead stroke, the bird is stroked from over the head or right shoulder, at full reach of the arm and racket. In fact, the player should *stretch* for the bird, even to the point of raising up on the tip of his toes. For this reason, the overhead stroke should be reserved for the higher flights, that is, the "pop-ups" and the High Clears. The resulting flights from this stroke should be confined to a Smash, Drop, or High Clear.

The only difference between the overhead stroke as used to produce a Smash and a Drop is that in the case of the Drop, the stroke is checked as the racket passes over the head and is gauged so as to direct the bird just over and close to the net. The advanced player will usually introduce deception in the case of the Drop by faking a Smash. The overhead is the most offensive stroke in badminton when used for a Smash—it is, therefore, used more often for the kill than any other stroke. Here is where the ambitious, energetic player may give full vent to his strength.

The Overhead Stance

When the player has decided to meet the bird with an overhead stroke and has maneuvered into stroking position, he should be standing with his left foot from 14 to 18 inches ahead of the right. The left foot is pointed in line with the oncoming bird. (Fig. 14) The weight of the body during the stroking movement is on the rear foot, except at the start and completion of the stroke.

Height of Bird-Racket Contact

As mentioned earlier, the point of bird-racket contact should be as high as the player can reach (preferably to the extent of reaching up on the tip of the toes). Further, this point should be about 18 to 24 inches directly out in front of the "body-head line." This will result in contacting the bird out in front of the body and directs the bird downward. In the early attempts with this stroke, special attention should be given to striking the bird downward.

Stance and Point of Contact

The usual error in the overhead stroke is one of judging the pace of the

Fig. 14: *The Overhand Stance*

oncoming bird, which results in an error in selection of the court spot for the overhead stance. The court spot for the overhead stance should be 12 to 18 inches back of the point at which the bird would hit the floor if permitted to fall. More precisely, this is the point where the left foot should be. (Note bird on the floor in Fig. 14.)

Practice will help the beginner develop the ability to judge the court spot which will give the proper contact point. He should have someone hit high birds to him, maneuvering into position as if to stroke, but allowing the birds to fall to the floor, and note the distance that they have fallen from his left foot. This will test the accuracy of judgment in selection of the spot for the stance. When he finds himself able to judge this spot correctly, he may then practice stroking the bird downward and from a full arm reach. Unless the bird is hit from a full arm reach and out in front of the head, power and deception in the stroke will be impossible.

In the beginning it will be noted that the tendency is to select a court spot too close to the net; that is, the player will run or step forward too far, or he will not get far enough back of the bird when going back for it. An oncoming flight thus poorly judged results in missing the bird entirely or in hitting it *directly* overhead for a weak return.

How to Stroke from Overhead

As in the forehand and backhand strokes, the player should start the backswing of the racket as he takes the stroking stance, so as to have plenty of time for a full swing without hurrying the stroke. In the backswing, the racket is dropped down at the back to a perpendicular position. The advanced player frequently leans backward, on the tip of his toes, to get a longer sweep and "more body" back of the swing.

Most of the power is applied to the stroke on the upswing of the racket—it is not, as the beginner often supposes, delayed until the racket is swung downward at the completion of the stroke. The advanced player makes this upswing with such terrific speed that he raises himself to the very tip of his toes—even off the floor. However, he does not jump for the bird. Jumping is definitely to be avoided.

The wrist-snap is not difficult to learn in the case of the overhead stroke. For a wrist-snap, the wrist must maintain a *lead* in front of the racket. As the wrist passes overhead, it is "snapped" so as to bring the racket face quickly ahead of the wrist. This "adds a movement" to that of the swing itself. In the wrist-snap, the racket face will come forward and downward faster if the "flick" is introduced (that is, if the wrist is suddenly withdrawn) just before the contact.

A slight turning of the racket from the wrist, just before the bird is struck, is of course necessary in order to hit the bird with the flat face of the racket. The bird must be contacted with the face of the racket flat to avoid slicing, and thus checking the speed of flight. CAUTION: DO NOT ALTER THE GRIP, or permit the racket to slip around in the hand. This is a common fault with the beginner and seems to be associated with the tendency to hit the bird too late and at a point close to the head level, instead of at the height of the reach. As he brings his racket into position for the stroke thus poorly timed, the player will invariably alter his grip instead of turning the racket at the wrist. Stroking low encourages a change in the grip and makes a fast downward flight impossible.

Summary of Action in the Overhead Stroke

1. Estimate the direction and angle of flight, and pace of the bird.

2. With this decision, select the court spot for the overhead stance and proceed *quickly* to that spot.

3. Assume the overhead stance, at a spot 12 to 18 inches back of the point at which it is estimated the bird would fall. (This is the position from which the bird may be hit out in front of the head by stretching the arm and racket full length.)

4. Begin the backswing of the racket as the stance is assumed.

5. Bring the racket back so that it is pointing down perpendicularly, behind the body.

6. Put the body back of the swing—lean back if you have sufficient control. Get to the court spot soon enough so there is time for a calculated stroke—but *don't hurry the stroke.*

7. Apply the power on the upward swing, keeping the wrist in advance until it is overhead.

8. As the bird approaches close to the contact point (the wrist should be overhead at this moment), "snap" the wrist, bringing the racket-face suddenly in advance of the wrist at the moment before the bird is hit.

9. DO NOT ALTER THE GRIP.

All this may sound complicated but the main thing involved is accuracy of timing and proper footwork (which is more or less true of all strokes, but especially the overhead). Since this stroke will be used mostly in returning the High Clear flights, there will usually be some time for deliberation, except when caught out of position. One important point to remember is that the High Clear flights, falling from considerable height, are deceiving and need to be judged with care.

IV. The Net Strokes

Aside from the strategic use of net play (placement to a weak court spot, playing for an opening, etc.), the net strokes are used to return the bird that falls very close to the net.

In the net strokes, the object is to return the bird so that it will barely clear the net and fall very close to the net on the other side. This calls for a delicate touch, since the stroke is of just sufficient force to "lift" the bird over the net or to direct it cross-court. Restraint, therefore, characterizes the net strokes. This is in sharp contrast to the freedom, power, and wrist flexibility requisite for the forehand, backhand, and overhead strokes.

Beginners usually find the net strokes relatively easy. They are, nevertheless, one of the most effective weapons of offense. At the same time, the suspense and thrill of net play, where the bird barely clears or actually touches the top of the net, and falls over the net to the other side, adds greatly to the fun of the game. Audiences delight in clever net play.

Types of Net Play

There are three distinct types of net play: (1) "Rushing"—meeting an upward flight which clears the net sufficiently to be returned with a quick Smash

Fig. 15: *Rushing*

or Drop near the net tape (Fig. 15); (2) the "lift" stroke, in which the bird is stroked down low (Fig. 16); and (3) a carefully gauged, high forehand (or backhand) stroke, in which the bird is stroked near and directed along the net tape to the opposite alley (Fig. 17). From the "lift" stroke, the short hairpin type of flight is commonly produced; from the other stroke, the cross-court flight is the result.

Of course the cross-court as well as the short hairpin flight may be produced with the lift stroke; but where the player wishes to make a quick cross-court placement and the time element does not force him to stroke low, he should strive to meet the bird as close to the net as possible. A short flight, directly over the net, may of course be produced from near the height of the net tape also. Variations as between the short and cross-court flight from either of these strokes provide interesting opportunities for deceptive tactics, as for example, faking a cross-court flight to one alley and "dropping" the bird just over the net to the opposite alley. This and other obvious variations of deceptive play are relatively easy at the net.

Fig. 16: *The "Lift" Stroke*

In "rushing" the net, care must be taken to avoid touching the net or hitting the bird before it crosses over, both of which constitute a fault.

Stance for the Net Strokes

The choice between the right or left foot forward for the stroking stance at the net will often depend on the player's court position. Hence, no definite rules need be set down. When stroking from the right side of the court, the player is better prepared to cover the unguarded court area (on his left) if his right foot is forward. The right foot forward also tends to lengthen the reach, thus enabling the player to keep a safer distance from the net. Then too, net play involves short flights and placements to a considerable extent, forcing the opponent to hurry and the stroker to guard against a possible net return to either alley.

Fig. 17: Cross-Court Stroke at the Net

(1)

(2)

(3)

Fig. 17: *Cross-Court Stroke at the Net*

How to Stroke at the Net

In the "lift" stroke, the bird-racket contact is made with the racket practically parallel to the floor. (See Fig. 16) At the moment of contact, the grip is firmed so as to provide a solid surface from which the bird may be *delicately* directed. The racket movement of the stroke consists primarily of a "lift" rather than a swinging movement from the wrist. The lift, with a rigid wrist rather than a flexible wrist stroke, is best suited for the accuracy required for the short net flight. Many points are scored in the usual game from "pop-ups" at the net, resulting from poorly executed net strokes. "Pop-ups" are usually the result of swinging at the bird rather than "lifting" it carefully.*

In stroking cross-court, a gentle "gate swing" from the wrist and partly from the elbow is used. (See Fig. 17) Note that at the beginning of the stroke the racket face is nearly flat and parallel with the floor. This permits "lifting" the bird directly over the net if the situation calls for a short hairpin flight, and also disguises the player's intent. The cross-court stroke should be made from as close to the net tape as possible.

---

*The "lift" stroke constitutes a "distinct hit" as defined by the rules. It is not in any sense a "throw" as discussed in Chapter III. (See Rule No. 14, page 34.)

Common Faults in the Fundamental Strokes

1. Hurrying the stroke (not taking sufficient time for a full backswing).

2. Jumping for the bird.

3. Wrong stance (e.g., left foot forward for backhand).

4. Stroking the bird too close to the body, thus hampering the racket swing (usually the result of overrunning, or in the case of the overhead, permitting the bird to fall too low).

5. Failure to "finger" the grip.

6. Failure to keep the eyes on the bird at time of contact.

7. "Pushing" the bird (using the whole arm rather than the wrist).

8. Contacting the bird with the racket face at an incorrect angle (results in slicing, cutting, or lofting the bird).

9. Locked or humped wrist.

10. A late or inadequate windup.

11. Poor footwork (late arrival at court spot for the stance).

12. Using a wrist action in the lift stroke at the net.

13. Not firming the grip for an overhead drop or for a net stroke.

14. Rigid wrist.

15. Lack of thought action (not thinking the steps through).

16. Racket turning in the hand, thus altering the grip.

CHAPTER VII

Footwork

Proper footwork is one of the most important essentials for good stroking. The court area is small, and the game as played by the experts is fast. Footwork is directly related to stroking in that the player slow in maneuvering into position must hurry his stroke to make up for this loss of time. In other words, he will not have sufficient time for the full windup and backswing essential for a good stroke. Stance is of course a part of footwork. The stroking stances, which are a completion of the footwork, were treated in connection with the strokes and need not be discussed further. There is, however, one other stance to consider—the "on-guard" stance, which is the position assumed when *waiting* for the bird to be hit by the opponent.

The On-Guard Stance

For the alert on-guard stance, the body is bent slightly forward and the weight is fairly evenly distributed on the two feet. The feet may be from 14 to 18 inches apart, while the left foot is a little ahead of the right and pointing in the direction of the opponent who is about to hit the bird. (Fig. 18) The knees

Fig. 18: *The On-Guard Stance*

should be flexed slightly so as to bring the heels barely off the floor and to distribute most of the weight on the toes and ball of the feet. This stance permits the quickest action toward or away from the net or in any other direction. About 90% of all directional movements of the player are toward and away from the net.

Note in the illustration of the on-guard stance (Fig. 18) how the racket is carried. In so holding the racket, the player is prepared to receive a quick Smash or Drive to either side of the body. In this connection, remember that the net is five feet high and that you will be standing only 9 or 10 feet away from it a good share of the time. The time lost in bringing the racket up from a low position is therefore an important factor.

The Pivot

Quick movements to the right or left or completely about face are most easily made with a "pivot." The ball and toes of the foot act as the pivot or turning point. The foot on the side to which the body is turned is the pivoting foot. The other foot serves to balance the body and to "push off." The pivoting movement, however, is begun and directed by the head and shoulders.

Beginners frequently find themselves awkward in pivoting simply because they fail to realize that the movement begins with the head and shoulders rather than with the feet. An easy, natural pivot may be made from the on-guard position. This is because the head and shoulders are already forward in the position best suited to turning or "throwing" the body around. The quick start so necessary for BETTER BADMINTON depends to a considerable extent on the use of the pivot. A player slow in turning to the right or left rarely arrives at the proper court spot in time to make a good stroke.

Movements Away from the Net

Pivoting is especially important for returns which require a sudden movement or retreat directly from the net. The frequency of this directional movement has already been mentioned. The common tendency in this situation is to "back up." Such a movement is too clumsy and slow. Instead of backing up, pivot quickly to the right or left (depending on the side of the bird flight) and take the necessary steps *forward*. The stroke may then be made from the normal stroking stance (i.e., left foot forward for the forehand, and right foot forward for the backhand) by simply turning the body in the direction of the bird and bringing the proper foot forward. The problem in footwork is how to get into the position best suited for stroking and at the same time maintain balance. This has a definite bearing on the return stroke which follows the one immediately in question, since good balance is essential for recovery and preparedness for the next stroke.

With good footwork, the player may also minimize his weaker backhand returns in favor of his forehand. In the return of long, high flights, experts are frequently seen making a quick pivot to the left and circling completely around the bird in order to avoid a backhand. Basil Jones, exhibitionist superb and international pro, is an excellent exponent of this pivot and style of maneuvering to the backcourt.

The pivot and *forward* movement to the backcourt may sound to the beginner like a procedure even slower than backing up, but such is not the case. The on-guard position enables the player to make the pivot and start away from the net very quickly. The important difference between this method and that of backing away from the net is the resulting balance and position (or stance) for stroking. The pivot enables the player to maneuver into the position best suited to a full-sweeping, strong return. By backing away he will find himself off balance and forced to strike the bird from behind his body or with a shorter stroke, resulting in a weak return. Further, because he is off balance, he will be unable to recover quickly for the next return.

Covering Court

Short, quick steps rather than long strides are best suited to movements in any direction. They permit a quicker stopping and turning, and correction of position in relation to the bird when misjudgments occur. Jack Purcell's footwork, which is of course an outstanding model, is particularly noticeable for this fact.

Movements should be avoided as much as possible while the opponent is about to stroke the bird, since he is looking for the opportunity to catch you off balance by placing the bird in the spot from which you are moving.

When the bird is in play, the player should, whenever possible, take up a position in the center of the court area for which he is responsible. This area may be designated the "home position."* When forced to leave his home position, the player should return to it after he has stroked the bird, if time permits. This gives him the quickest access to all points of the area for which he is responsible. There will of course be some exceptions to this rule in certain

---

*This position is aptly termed "home plate" by Leon Ketchum. See "Badminton"—(Chicago Park District—Modern Recreation Series—1937).

systems of teamwork. The on-guard stance should be assumed as one takes up this position.

Footwork Illustrated

In the four illustrations comprising Figure 19, the shaded portions near the center of the court represent the home position or spots from which easiest access may be gained to all points of the court area for which the player is responsible. This is the spot to which the player should return for the on-guard position after completing each stroke, if time permits of course. In any event, he should get as near to this spot as possible,** *before* the opponent strokes. (Moving as the opponent strokes of course leaves an opening for a placement to catch you off balance. You are in an awkward position to receive the bird placed at the side or spot from which you are moving.)

Since most of the directional movements are toward or away from the net, the player is always facing the net in the on-guard stance, and one foot (the left) is forward. The feet are never side by side, except in the case of the net player in mixed doubles (when the up-and-back system of teamwork is used). Where play is thus confined to the net area, the movements will be mostly to either side and forward, never to the backcourt.

Figure 19a illustrates the footwork involved in making a simple forehand and backhand in a singles or mixed doubles game. To reach a bird flying to his right, the player pushes off with the left foot and pivots to the right, bringing the left foot to the footprint marked No. 1; he then brings the right foot to print No. 2 and the left to No. 3—at this point he is in position for the forehand stroke. To reach a bird flying to his left, he pushes off with his right foot, pivots on the left, brings the right foot to No. 1, then the left to No. 2 and the right to No. 3—at this point he is in position for the backhand stroke.

While we speak of "pushing off" with one foot and "pivoting" on the other, it should be repeated that the pivoting movement is begun and directed by the head and shoulders. This is one reason why the player should never straighten up to look at the bird as it passes overhead. This leaves him flat-footed and unable to pivot quickly. He should, instead, lose no time in making the pivot and moving toward the backcourt. The speed, direction, and angle of flight, perceived immediately after the bird is struck, are sufficient to judge its course without waiting. This is not to say that the eyes should not be kept

---

**An exception should be noted: When your opponent has been forced into a weak court position, you would not of course return "home," but rather go to the net so as to take advantage of the anticipated weak return.*

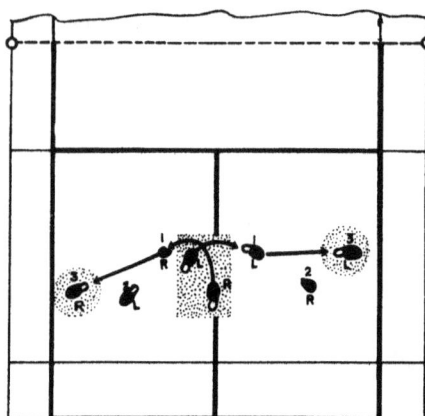

(a) Forehand and backhand return

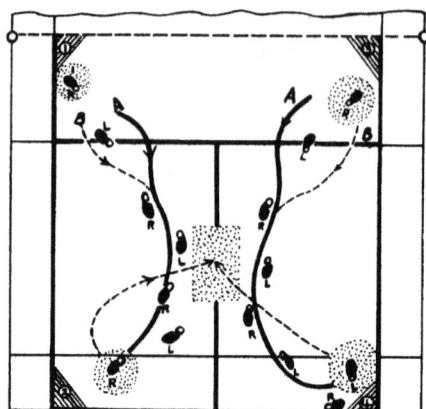

(b) Backcourt return

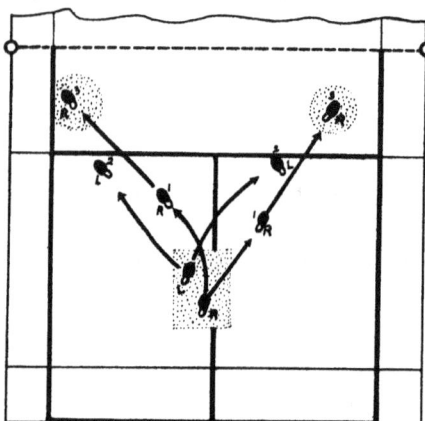

(c) Net return

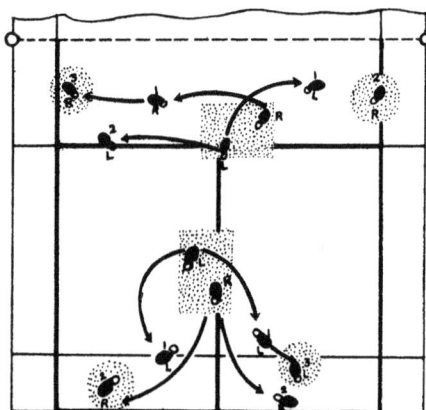

(d) Footwork in "Up-and-Back" combination

Fig. 19: Footwork Illustrated

on the bird, but rather to stress the importance of the body and head position for pivoting. Other than in making the about-face pivot, when the bird is overhead and still ascending, remember to *keep the eye on the bird.*

Figure 19b illustrates the footwork involved in getting to the backcourt to return a clear, immediately following a return at the net in a singles game. The player has just returned a bird directed to the corner marked No. 1, or to that marked No. 3. His opponent clears this return to the back corner directly opposite, that is, to points No. 2 or 4. Since the bird will be passing between the player and the alley (overhead, of course), the tendency will be to pivot to that side, that is, toward "B" and in the direction indicated by the dotted lines. However, a pivot toward "A," and in the direction indicated by the solid lines, is preferred. In either case, the circling movement is begun immediately after the about-face pivot, and the player makes his way to a position for the return stroke (backhand in the one case and forehand in the other). After the return stroke is made from the backcourt, the player takes up the on-guard position in the center of the court. (The lines in this illustration indicate the movement of the body rather than the feet.)

Figure 19c illustrates the footwork (in singles) in making a backhand and forehand return at the corner of the net. The same principles are involved as in the other two cases—a pivot to the left or right, with the necessary forward steps to the stroking position. Figure 19d shows the footwork of the "up" player and the "back" player in a mixed doubles combination. The situations vary slightly from those shown in the other illustrations. The principles are the same, however, and no further comment is necessary.

Patterns of "Thought Action"

To effect a combination of good footwork and stroking form into a well-coordinated whole, definite patterns of thought and action need to be developed. By this is simply meant that the player must form in his mind certain definite associations which will quickly call forth the proper muscular reaction to the particular situation at hand. This thinking process and the action which results may be termed a "pattern of thought and action" or simply "thought action." It is believed that this point will become clearer in the discussion which follows. This is not an attempt to make the subject unnecessarily involved or technical. But the recognition of this principle of "thought action" and its application to the game of badminton is of great importance to the person who wishes to become proficient in the game. This principle of "thought action" of course applies equally well to any other game.

Thought Action as Applied to the Return

The thought or visualization of what is happening must necessarily precede the action or response to this mental "sizing up" of the situation. As applied to a bird already in play, this means that the player, having decided toward which side of the body the bird is approaching and hence where it is to be met, is prepared to pivot and turn toward the "ideal court spot." The ideal court spot is that spot on the court from which the return stroke may be best executed. On the selection of this, and of course, on the correct anticipation of the bird's flight, depends the freedom of the body, arm and wrist in stroking. In other words, the ideal court spot gives the proper distance between the bird and player for this freedom of action. On the latter, in turn, depend the timing, accuracy, and strength of return.

Sequence of Thought Action

The thought action patterns which must be developed for BETTER BADMINTON may thus be considered to contain three factors or steps. These involve a decision as to (1) the direction in which the bird is approaching, (2) the side of the body on which the bird must be received, and (3) how to maneuver the feet and body into the stroking position best suited to promote ease, grace, accuracy, and power.

Each of these steps must be decided in the order mentioned, and very quickly. It is of course a matter of split seconds. Nevertheless, the process as described is there and its divisions distinct. To recognize this fact, and to make use of it, is a start on the road to BETTER BADMINTON.

The attempt to "think out," as it were, one's actions will seem awkward at first, perhaps even more so than a blind pursuit of the elusive bird, with dependence on chance alone. But the end result will be quite the other way. In the skilled player thought action has been developed to such a fine degree that the action appears purely mechanical. To the beginner too it will become "mechanical," if he makes a definite attempt to start the development of these patterns through practice.

BETTER BADMINTON places a premium on speed of thought and accurate decisions. The player should not attempt to wait for decisions on all three steps before starting into action. This is precisely where the beginner most commonly errs. Start the required action immediately after the first step has been decided upon. This immediate start conserves the starting time required to make the first step; and it allows for thinking through the next step and making that decision while the action required for completion of the first decision is being carried out. Beginners seem slow on their feet because they often attempt to think through all three of the steps before going into action. The result is a weak return or complete failure to return.

Thought Action at Work

Obviously, as already suggested, each thought action requires a decision preceding the action. The striking of the bird by the opponent should be followed immediately by a quick decision as to the side on which the bird is to be received. Then the player pivots immediately in that direction, throwing his weight forward and swinging his head in the general direction that his decision has indicated the bird will fly. In the meantime, while his legs are carrying him toward the "ideal court spot," the thought processes are at work deciding how far away from the body the bird will pass. This court spot is the next place of destination to which his legs are carrying him. In order to permit freedom of the body, arm, and wrist, the player should be careful to select this ideal spot (or in other words, he must come to a stop) four or more feet from the aerial point where the bird is about to pass the body—i.e., at nearly full reach of the arm and racket.

Thought Actions of the Champion

Forming these thought and action patterns in their respective sequence permits a gracefulness and rapidity of body movement. They also reduce the physical and mental strain during the time the player is moving from his original position to where he should receive the bird. Champions such as Purcell, Kramer, Devlin, Davidson, Willard, and others are characterized by the speed of their thought actions. This gives them the tremendous advantage of conserved time and eases the strain of competitive badminton. Herein lies part of the secret of the champion's strategy. It is this "added time," fraction of a second though it be, that enables him to plan his strategic moves. The difference between him and his less skilled opponent is, to a considerable extent, this difference.

Common Faults in Footwork

1. Carrying the racket down and at the side while in the on-guard position.
2. Throwing the head up and running backward (instead of pivoting) to return flights overhead and out of reach.
3. Maneuvering too close to the bird.
4. Getting too close to the net in net play. (Stop with the rear foot on or very close to the short service line.)
5. Slow in starting.
6. Failure to use the feet and body sufficiently (relying entirely on the arms to do the work).
7. Failure to recover balance and position after stroke.
8. Failure to develop patterns of thought action.
9. Failure to keep the eyes on the bird.

CHAPTER VIII

The Service in Singles and Doubles*

Unlike the server in tennis, the server in badminton is on the defensive. The Rules Committee has considered the serve as a means of putting the bird into play rather than as an offensive measure. Hence the rule: "It is a fault if the service is overhand," that is, if the bird is struck above the waist (or hand holding the racket). This means that the server is hitting *upward*, since the height of the net is five feet and that of the hips around three feet. This means further that the bird must have a rise of at least two feet in a distance of about nine feet, to reach its apex of flight at the net. Hitting *up* under any circumstances, and especially in the service, places the player on the defensive.

The rule against an "overhand" service is logical since the distance involved is so short that an "overhand" service would be entirely too offensive, both literally and otherwise.

But the low service places the server in a "bad spot" *if it is not executed accurately*, and there are no rules as to the severity of a return. For this reason, the technique of the service is a very important fundamental.

In Chapter II we considered only the simplest type of serve. However, the situations in singles and doubles play are quite different and normally call for two distinct types of serve. In the *singles* game, the server is not only on the defensive but he is responsible for the entire court area. For this reason he will normally use a *long, high* flight (i.e., a High Clear to the backcourt) instead of a short flight such as was described in Chapter II. The reason for this is found in the fact that the long, high flight of the advanced player's serve is normally about 30 feet high and 30 feet long. This gives him time to "get set" for the return, and of course forces the receiver to *wait*. The waiting, and the fact that the bird is falling of its own weight, tend to present the receiver with timing difficulties. The reader will readily appreciate this point after he has received one or two serves of the type described. The long, high serve thus tends to equalize the positions of the two players in a situation which is otherwise in favor of the receiver.

The *short* serve, which is commonly used in *doubles*, is merely a refinement of the simple serve described in Chapter II. While it is primarily a "doubles serve," it is adequate, with certain modifications, for the beginner's use in singles until he has gained the control and stroking power requisite for

---

*A large part of this chapter, in somewhat different form, appeared as an article, entitled "Badminton—A Co-Recreational Sport," in "Scholastic Coach"—April, 1938.

a long, high serve. Because of the simplicity of the short serve and because the doubles game is the more frequently played for sociability, we recommend that the beginner seek proficiency in the short before attempting the long, high service.

A toss delivery, in place of the out-of-hand delivery, should be learned as soon as the necessary proficiency is developed. The delay in stroking occasioned by a toss delivery has the advantage of better concealing the server's intentions. In other words, the point of placement of the serve and the fact of whether the serve is to be long or short, is left longer in doubt. However, besides the matter of timing there is another disadvantage to the toss as against the out-of-hand—the bird is ordinarily hit down lower and hence at a sharper upward angle, which presents greater danger of popping up.

Types of Serve

The serves, then, may be classified according to the type of flight, as follows: (1) the short serve, (2) the long serve, which may be further divided into two types, (a) the high serve, and (b) the driven serve.

The short serve, as we indicated in Chapter III (Bird Flight), is a very carefully calculated and measured cross-court flight, with the bird clearing the net by less than three inches and directed to a point a trifle inside the short service line. The High Serve is a high clear type of flight while the Driven Serve is simply a driven flight. (See Figs. 9 and 20) Both of the long serves should be directed to a vulnerable corner in the backcourt.

While the short serve is primarily a "doubles" serve and the long, high serve is primarily a "singles" serve, this does not mean that they are confined to either game. The most we can say is that the short serve is used in about 80% of the serves in doubles matches, and that the long, high serve is used in about 80% of the serves in singles matches. In either type of game, the two serves will be alternated occasionally to catch the receiver off-guard, if he proves capable of coping with the serve ordinarily suited to the occasion. It is a cardinal rule of the game never to "change a winning game." Obviously, it would be foolish to change to a short serve if the opponent is having difficulty with your long serve, and vice versa.

The Short Serve

The only difference between the short serve as presented here and the simple serve as presented in Chapter II'is that we are now establishing more precise rules as to court position and placement in order to achieve greater accuracy. A high degree of accuracy is necessary because, as we said a moment ago, the server is hitting up and is therefore on the defensive. Thus, it is necessary when using the short serve to calculate the flight carefully—to keep the bird very close to the net tape, and to keep it out of easy reach of the opponent —to avoid placing oneself at too great a disadvantage. At the same time, the service should be made from as high as is legally possible. The greater the height at which the bird is hit, the less will be the upward angle or rise to the flight.

This ideal short service flight has been referred to in badminton circles as a "falling bird flight"; that is, the bird begins falling as soon as it crosses the net. A rising bird flight or "pop-up" is to be avoided since it gives the receiver a "set-up," that is, leaves the server open to a rush and Smash return. There is no secret to this technique of a "falling bird flight." It simply requires: (1) correct selection of court positions for serving, i.e., exactly a racket's length from the short service line, (2) accurate placement, (3) a delicately executed stroke, and (4) the proper bird-racket contact, i.e., as high as legally permitted and with the racket face at right angles to the floor.

Court Positions for the Service in Singles and Doubles

Court Positions for the service in singles and doubles should differ for both offensive and defensive reasons. In doubles, service should be made from either of the footprints or court-spots marked (1) and (2) in Figure 20. Spot No. 1 is selected when a wide cross-court angle of flight is desired. In either position, the server should stand exactly a racket's length back of the short service line. Maintaining this distance at all times will establish such factors as upward angle and distance of flight, and gauging of stroke, as fixed habits. A *racket's length* is stressed because the desired upward angle of flight and "a falling bird flight" are most easily attained from this distance.

In the *right court*, spot No. 1 gives a wider selection for placement than does spot No. 2. In fact, from this angle in the right court the server may conveniently reach all four corners of the receiving court with a fair degree of safety. It will be a particularly effective service position if the receiver proves vulnerable to placements to the inside back corner (point L-1a in Fig. 20a).

Because of the angle, spot No. 2 (midway between the alley and midcourt line) offers less selection for placements in the right court. Hence, from this position the server will ordinarily need a more deceptive* serve if he is going to

---

*"Deception," as used in this connection, should not be confused with "feinting." The latter is not permissible in the serve. By using "deception" we mean using the element of surprise—in this instance, serving to the unexpected point.

vary his service at all and keep within safe bounds. Of course, definite and unchangeable rules for position (and placement) in serving cannot be established—at least, the smart server will not prescribe such limits for himself. Weaknesses in your opponents will naturally vary so that what proves to be a smart tactic against one will not necessarily be so against another. The player should test his opponent for his receiving weaknesses at an early stage of the game and plan his service strategy accordingly.

The left court presents a more difficult service problem than does the right court. The left court player (except in mixed doubles) is ordinarily expected to cover all forehands and overheads within his reach, in order to avoid the weaker backhand returns of the right court player. For this reason the server in the left court will ordinarily use a spot corresponding to No. 1 less often than No. 2 because it places him too far out of position. Then too, the selection for placements in the left court (See Fig. 20) are more limited than in the right court. By standing nearer the center of his service court, the left court server is better prepared to vary his placements from points S-1 and S-2. (See Fig. 20) For example, being close to the receiver, he is in a better position to make an occasional quick placement to the inside back corner (not numbered on Fig. 20) which would be a dangerous tactic from the alley service position. This threat tends to keep the receiver from covering the backhand corner (point S-1) as well as he might otherwise do.

In either court, spot No. 2 is the usual selection by the man when playing mixed doubles because it enables him to cover a larger court area for the return.

The footprints marked No. 3 show the singles service position, which should always be as close to the midcourt line as possible (keeping the foot off the midcourt line) and a little farther back from the short service line than the doubles service positions. This distance is ideally a racket's length plus about 18 inches, which of course places the server nearer to the center of the court. However, until the necessary strength of stroke is developed, and for a better defense against a quick drop flight in return, it may be necessary to serve a little closer to the short service line at first.

Placement Points for the Service in Singles and Doubles

The server should aim his services at certain points on the receiver's court. In the court diagrams (Fig. 20), first choice for the short service placement is labeled S-1 and S-1a. This placement forces the receiver to hit *up* from his backhand. Point S-1 has a further advantage when serving from the alley position in the right court—at the start of the stroke, it is difficult for the receiver to judge whether the flight will be short or long, i.e., directed to S-1 or L-1a.

73

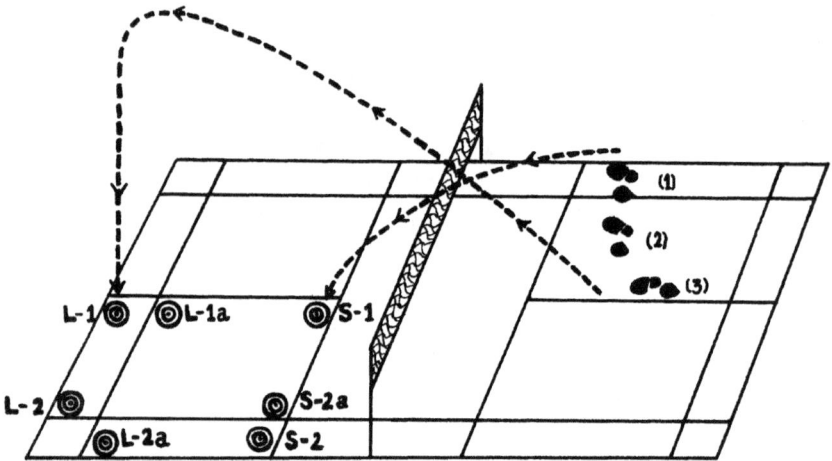

(a) Right court

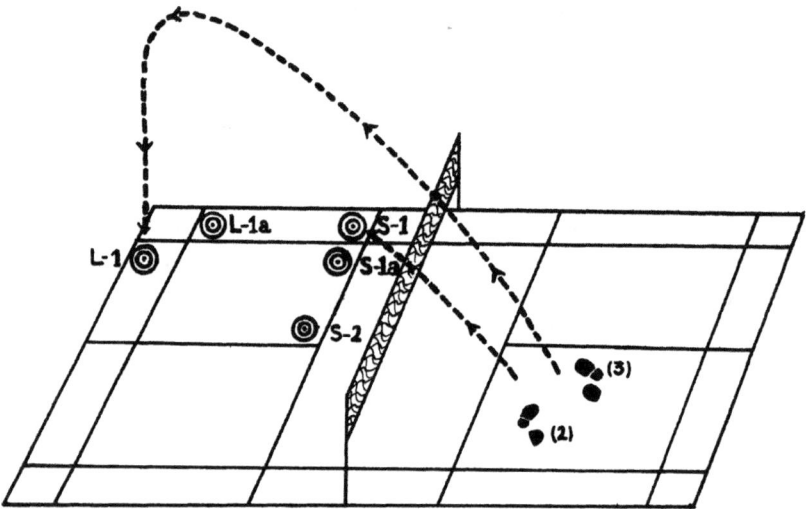

(b) Left court

Fig. 20: Court Positions and Placement Points in the Serve

(L-1a is an effective placement in doubles and may be reached with a driven flight.)

The placement points for the high service (No. L-1 and L-1a) are selected so as to direct the play to the receiver's backhand and to his overhead weaknesses. In the right half-court, two other placement points are very effective—the outside corner labeled L-2 and L-2a. Serving to this corner of course tends to force the receiver out of position and allows the server to take command. Variations from one to the other of the placement points shown, or even to other points, will of course be made to catch the receiver off-guard. For example, if his racket is being held low, a quick placement to his shoulder will often be effective.

As already suggested, in the right half-court, the point marked L-1a is also a very effective placement in doubles, as a variation from the placements to points S-1 and S-2. This point may be reached very easily with a driven flight from the out-of-hand service. (A toss is not necessary to reach this point when the driven flight is used.) It is apparent from Fig. 20 that this flight, directed from court spot No. 1, is not only to the receiver's backhand but is of such an angle that it crosses well over the left court and is not within easy reach of the receiver.*

One should never make his service to the forehand (point S-2) obvious. Every effort should be made to conceal the intended placement, but the rule is particularly important when serving to the receiver's strength. Look at the opponent before serving to pick out the point of best possible vantage. It should be borne in mind that one object in the service is to force the receiver to move—as you attempt to do in your return flights.

The Short Service Stance

In Chapter II we showed only one stance—with the left foot forward. Figure 21 shows two slightly varying stances for the short service. There is some controversy over the relative merits of a right or left-foot-forward stance. The type of stance shown here is used more frequently by the advanced player in combination with a toss. There are two arguments advanced for a right-foot-forward stance: (1) it permits a quicker pivot or movement to return birds from a backhand, and is particularly appropriate for the right court alley position where the receiver is otherwise clearly out of position for a backhand return; (2) it does not place the body in the way of the stroke. As to body

---

*Except when the player has developed a " 'round-the-head" stroke for receiving high flights to his backhand.

(a) Left foot forward

(b) Right foot forward

Fig. 21: *The Short Service Stance*

interference, the position of the body itself in relation to the arm is perhaps more important than which foot is forward.

An argument for the left foot forward, on the other hand, is that one is in a stronger position for overhead play. For the short serve, we recommend the left-foot-forward stance to the beginner primarily because he is likely to find it more natural (as in golf or in batting, for example). For the out-of-hand serve, where little arm movement is used in the stroke, there is of course less possibility for interference of the body with the stroke than when a toss serve is used. In any event, the final decision should rest with the player, after he has experimented for himself.

Simplicity of the Short Serve

In spite of the exactness implied above, the short serve will come relatively easy to the beginner if he will make a point of practicing it apart from the game. It may be practiced off the court by marking the net height (five feet) on a wall and a line on the floor the same distance from the wall as the short service line is from the net (i.e., $6\frac{1}{2}$ feet). He should also assume what would be the normal court positions. The short service is easy for another reason already suggested: the court spots for the stance and the placement points remain uniform, thus enabling the player to fix the angle and distance of flight through habit. Therefore, no adjustments for new situations are necessary, as in the case of return strokes.

Summary of Thought and Action in the Short Serve

1. Select a court spot exactly a racket's length back of the short service line, and in the alley or between the alley and mid-court line.

2. Place the toe of the forward foot on this spot.

3. Assume the service stance—preferably with the left foot forward, unless you find the other stance easier or prefer it for other reasons.

4. Check the racket grip—remember that the racket face should be at right angles to the floor, as the bird is contacted.

5. For the out-of-hand serve, hold the tip of the bird-feathers with the tips of the index finger and thumb, and on a line with the wrist. For the toss serve, hold the cork between the index finger and thumb.

6. Judged from the position and weaknesses of the receiver, and other strategic considerations, make a choice for placement.

7. Having thus selected the direction of flight, adjust the stance to effect that direction, without making your intentions obvious.

8. Now focus the eye on the bird (and keep it there).

9. For an out-of-hand serve, direct the backswing of the racket from the wrist, as though the racket were a gate and the wrist a hinge. For a toss serve, toss the bird well out in front and a little to the side. In a tossed short serve, the stroke is similar to that of the long, high serve (see Fig. 23) except that less windup is necessary, and of course the stroke is much softer; for this reason, little or no flick, as described for the long, high serve (page 79), is necessary.

10. In the case of the out-of-hand serve, tap the bird lightly from the hand, firming the grip at the instant of impact. Whichever type of serve is used, take care to adjust the strength of the stroke for the precise amount of energy necessary to send the bird to the short service placement point.

The Long, High Serve

To summarize our earlier remarks on the long, high serve, it is used because: (1) it gives the singles server the necessary time to "get set" for the return, (2) forces the receiver to the backcourt, thus tending to place him out of position for the server's next play, (3) it keeps the opponent waiting—this, together with the fact that the bird is falling of its own weight from a height of 30 feet, makes it a difficult flight for him to judge and time; he may also be unable to clear from baseline to baseline.

The Long, High Service Stance

In the photo sequence of the long, high service (see Fig. 23), the right-foot-forward stance is shown. This is the stance more frequently used in this service by the experts, though not all of them by any means. The arguments pro and con for either stance were discussed in connection with the short serve. In general, those arguments apply here. However, the distinction between the two stances, so far as readiness for the return is concerned, is less apparent in the long, high serve since the server has more time to prepare himself. Some players advance still another argument for the right foot forward —that it permits the server to reach farther out in front of the body, making it easier to reach the backcourt with a high serve, without sacrificing court position.

It is interesting to note that two of the greatest players of all time differ on this matter of stance. Jack Purcell uses and strongly advocates the right-foot-forward stance. J. F. Devlin, on the other hand, uses and advocates the left-foot-forward stance.*

Delivery of the Toss

The method of holding the bird for a toss is another matter open to choice and on which there is some disagreement. There are two ways of holding the bird: (1) by the tip of the feathers, somewhat as in the out-of-hand delivery, except that the fingers are extended down the feather shaft slightly, and (2) by the cork, with the tip of the forefingers and thumb. (Fig. 22)

We recommend the latter since we feel that it makes for greater *accuracy in the toss.* By holding the cork, the bird may be thrown as though it were a dart. In any event, the bird should not be held by the glued part (i.e., the lower part of the feather shaft) since this is apt to be sticky and cause an inaccurate toss.

Fig. 22: *Holding the Bird—Toss Delivery*

Holding the bird high and tossing it up into the air is recommended since it gives time for a full windup and backswing, thus adding to the power of the stroke.

The Long, High Service Stroke

It will be observed that the stroke pictured here (Fig. 23) is a strong, circular underswing with much of the power coming from the wrist. The swing begins with the racket a little below the waist. The short forward swing at the start gives a longer windup and hence more power. The backswing is a full sweep with the face of the racket parallel to the line of movement. Observe the wrist lead in the down-swing of the racket (3rd photo) and note that the face of the racket is still parallel to the line of movement. As the racket passes the legs and to the front of the body, it is turned from the wrist to meet the bird with the flat face. The wrist lead is maintained until a moment before

*See: J. F. Devlin's "Badminton for All" (Doubleday Doran—1937).

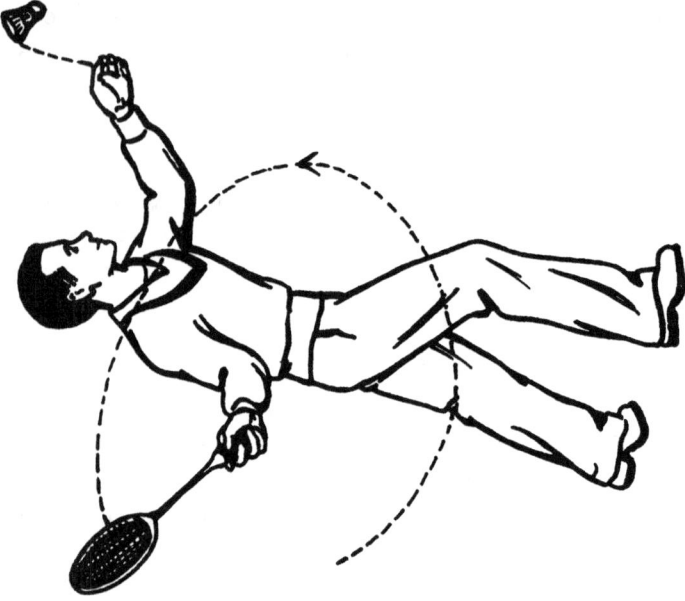

(2)

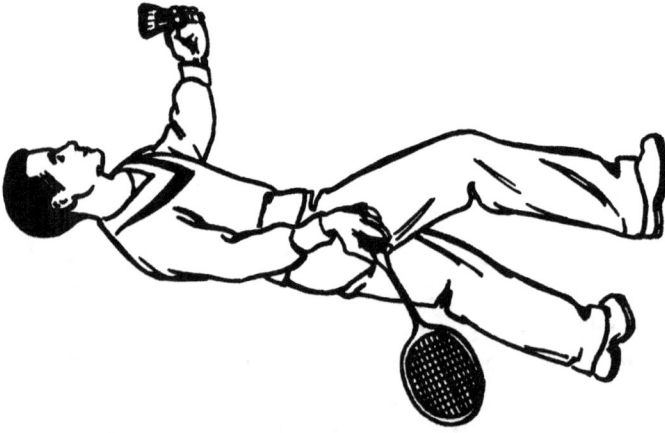

(1)

Fig. 23 : *The Long, High Service Stroke*

(4)

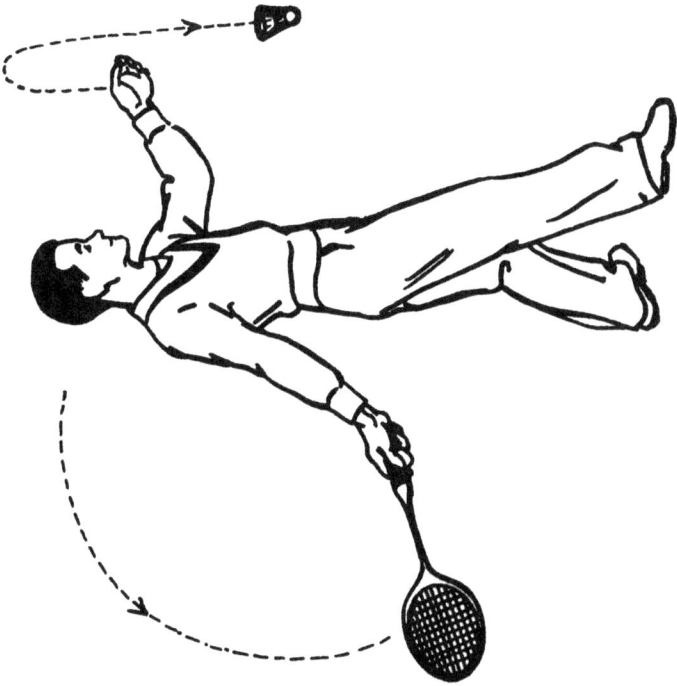

(3)

Fig. 23 (cont.) : *The Long, High Service Stroke*

81

the contact. Just before the contact the wrist is suddenly "snapped" and at the same time *withdrawn*. This "wrist-snap" and "flick" adds a movement to that of the racket swing itself. The dotted lines of the arm and racket in the last photo are intended to illustrate what actually happens in the flick.* A strong wrist action is necessary to get a high flight to the backcourt from the singles service position (i.e., a flight about 30 feet high and 30 feet long).

The Toss Serve in Doubles

The toss serve as used in doubles is similar to the serve just described. A powerful wrist-snap, however, is not required since the flights in this case are shorter. Less back-swing and a shorter toss will suffice for the short serve, the driven serve or a serve over the receiver's head. Some snap of the wrist is desirable, especially where the serve is directed to the back of the court.

The bird is tossed from approximately the level of the waist out in front and a little to the side. The proper amount of back-swing may be judged with a little practice. The snap is accomplished by allowing the wrist to lead the head of the racket in the forward-swing until a moment before contact. The head is then brought forward quickly by a snap of the wrist. The amount of

Fig. 24: *Stance for Receiving the Serve*

*Frequent references to the flick are made by Sir George Thomas, Bart., in his "Badminton" (Seeley, Service & Co., Ltd.—London—1936).

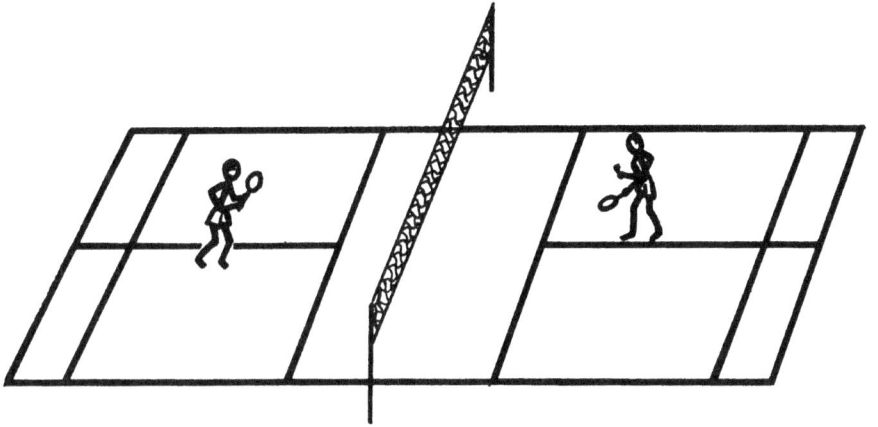

(a) Right court

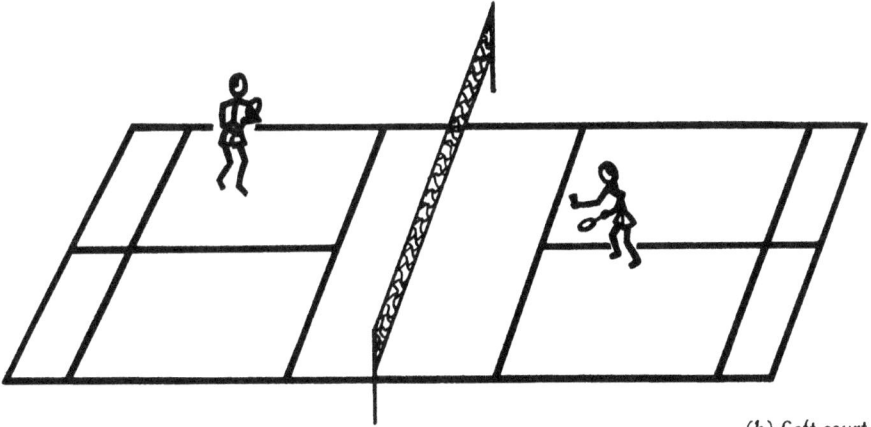

(b) Left court

Fig. 25. Position for Receiving the Serve—Singles

snap will be governed by the service flight desired. While the wrist-snap is not essential to an accurate toss serve it does enable the server to conceal his intentions more effectively.

Though we have given more prominence to the out-of-hand serve for doubles because of its simplicity, it should be the aim of every player to learn an accurate toss serve as early as possible since it can be made more effective and adds finesse to his game.

Receiving the Service

The stance (Fig. 24) for receiving a serve is similar to that of the on-guard stance. (Compare Fig. 24 with Fig. 18.) The *racket* is held *high* because, first of all, the net is five feet *high*. More specifically, this racket position enables the receiver to cover serves to the inside back corner with a 'round-the-head stroke. (Compare Fig. 24 with Fig. 36c.)

Court positions for receiving the service in singles are illustrated in Fig. 25. In the right court the receiver stands near the midcourt line and about midway between the short service line and the baseline. This enables him to cover most of the court with the forehand and serves to protect the vulnerable corner at the baseline and midcourt line. (See Fig. 20—Placement Points.) Flights to this outside corner will of course be to the backhand. In the left court (Fig. 25b) the receiver stands in what is approximately the center of the court. His chief concern is the vulnerable corner at the baseline and alley line. (See Fig. 20—Placement Points.)

The difference between the positions for doubles and singles is that the receiver stands closer to the short service line in receiving the doubles serve. The reasons for this are: (1) the court is 30 inches shorter, (2) most of the serves will be short (i.e., directed to the short service line), and (3) there is not the same need for concern over position for the next play (with a partner) if forced suddenly to the backcourt.

Common Service Faults

1. Too close to the net (not a racket's length from the short service line).
2. Assuming that the serve is *entirely* defensive.
3. Making the intended placement point obvious to the receiver.
4. Using the same court positions for singles and doubles.
5. Hurrying the service.
6. Serving *to* the receiver, that is, failing to serve where the best vantage lies.
7. Taking the eyes off the bird (watching the opponent while stroking rather than making decisions on placement before hitting the bird).
8. Making a high serve short of the backcourt.
9. Holding the glued part of the bird instead of the cork for a toss serve.
10. Inaccurate toss.
11. Out of position for receiving.
12. Carrying the racket low while receiving.

CHAPTER IX

Doubles Teamwork*

The fun of doubles will be greatly enhanced by successful teamwork. Successful teamwork requires that each player have a definite understanding of his responsibilities. In badminton there are four well known basic plans for division of these responsibilities. They are: (1) Side-by-side, (2) Up-and-

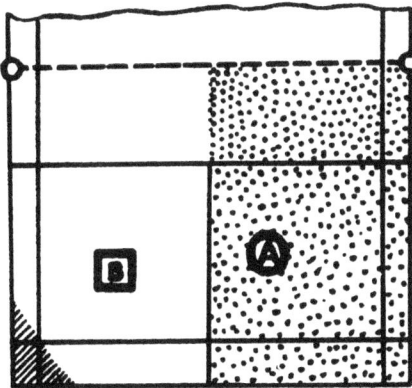

Side-by-side

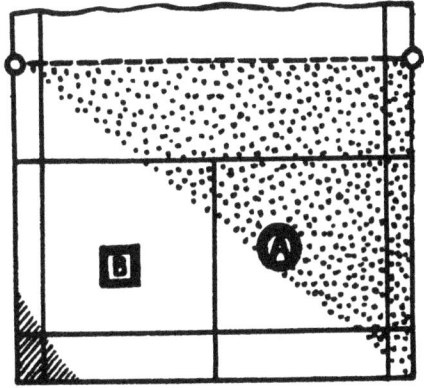

Diagonal

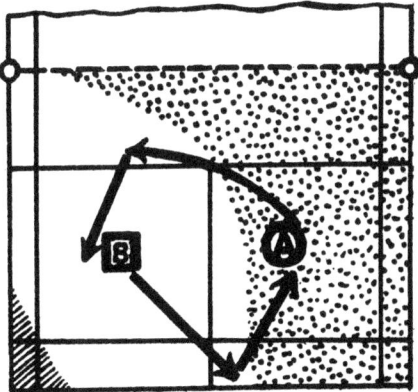

Rotation

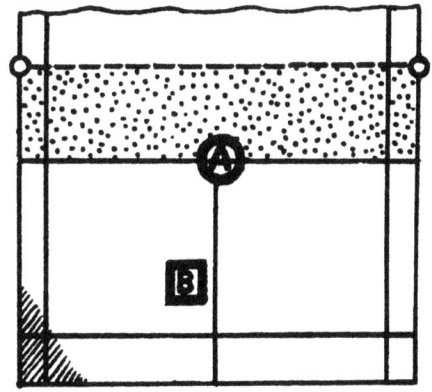

Up-and-Back

Fig. 26: *Teamwork*

---

*From: "Journal of Physical Education—Y.M.C.A."—July-August, 1938.

back, (3) Diagonal, and (4) Rotation. The division of responsibility in each case is indicated by the shaded and unshaded areas in the court drawings of Figure 26. The players should have a definite understanding so far as is possible, as to the type or combinations of these systems that shall in general be used. Some variations may of course be necessitated by circumstances.

The Side-By-Side System

In the side-by-side formation, the areas of responsibility are divided roughly according to an equal division of the court. This is the system most commonly used in men's or women's doubles when the abilities of the two players are equal or nearly so. Strictly speaking, the side-by-side is a defensive formation. Obviously, such a system is never adhered to rigidly, with neither player overstepping his half of the court. If one of the players is forced to the net, for example, the other becomes responsible for the backcourt—which is for the moment an up-and-back formation. Also, in any system of teamwork it is a generally recognized rule that you cover the net on your partner's smash. In the play following a return of the service, where one of the players takes the net, the diagonal or similar formation is usually resorted to for the moment. Further, it is a general rule that the left court player should return *all* overhead flights and forehands within his reach at the midcourt, rather than leave them for the backhand of his partner.

It is thus seen that a clear-cut division of the court as indicated in Figure 26 has the following disadvantages: (1) causes confusion at the midcourt, with the possibility of a clash of the partners or their rackets, (2) restricts the left court player in the use of his more powerful forehand, as a result of his partner's midcourt play, (3) makes it difficult to return overhead flights falling near the midcourt and backboundary lines of the right court, which are to the right court player's backhand, (4) leaves the backcourt unprotected when one of the players is forced to the net.

The Up-and-Back System

In the up-and-back system, which is the formation commonly used in mixed doubles, the responsibility is divided quite definitely. The "up" player restricts herself almost entirely to the area between the short service line and the net while the "back" player will only rarely go to the net. The most obvious disadvantage of this formation is that it places a heavy burden on the "back" player. Also, the players limit their experiences to specialized habits of play which do not carry over well into singles or other doubles formations.

86

The "up" player in a mixed doubles combination should only take those overhead flights which she can safely stroke for placement. This will ordinarily call for a quick drop or drive following a rush of "pop-ups." She will rarely have the time for the windup necessary for a hard smash. This is why the overhead play should ordinarily be left to the backcourt player. Indeed, her main concern is to direct her play so as to force the opponents to hit *up* to her partner. She should, therefore, never clear to the stronger partner on the opposing side. Another point for the net player to remember is never to back up into her partner's playing area.

In an up-and-back system of teamwork, there is the question of when the net player should take up her position in the net area following the service. This will depend on who is to assume responsibility for the net area immediately following the service, a point which needs to be definitely agreed upon before play. Ordinarily this responsibility rests with the receiver or server. There is no reason why this rule may not be followed in mixed doubles. In any case, the "up" player should take her position in the net area as soon after the return of service as possible. This position, as indicated in Figure 26, should be just ahead of the point of intersection of the midcourt and short service lines.

The Diagonal System

The diagonal system is a combination of the side-by-side and the up-and-back systems. It is the formation used ordinarily in the play immediately following service, where the server or receiver takes the net. As indicated in Figure 26, the right court player in a diagonal formation takes the net, leaving the left court player to protect the backcourt. It differs from the up-and-back system in that the backcourt player is not responsible for quite so large an area. The advantages of the diagonal system are apparent. In the diagram, B is responsible for a large part of the backcourt. Most overhead and right court plays will be taken by him since he is in position to deal with them more effectively. Its difficulty lies in the handling of flights directed to the extreme back corners of the court.

The Rotation System

The rotation system is so named because the players rotate their playing positions during the course of the game. As indicated by Figure 26, it is a combination of the other three systems. The arrows in the diagram illustrate the movement of the players when A is forced to the left side of the net. In this case, B moves over to the right court to guard the area for which A *was* responsible. As soon as A can safely leave the net, he moves back into the position formerly occupied by B. The rotation may be in either direction and may be started by either player. The fact that one player is forced out of his original court is the signal for the other to rotate, if necessary. The playing formation is otherwise similar to side-by-side.

The rotation system meets most of the objections to the other systems. Besides, it makes for a more even distribution of the play and more variety for both players. On the other hand, it presupposes equal playing ability in the partners in all departments of the game.

Points Requiring Special Agreement

There are certain points of weakness in any system of teamwork, and special agreement between the partners will be necessary to cover them. They include such matters as:

1. Covering a short return of the service.
2. Covering the net immediately after delivery of the service.
3. Covering overhead flights and low Drives down the center of the court.
4. Covering the net on partner's Smash.
5. Teaming of a left-handed player with a right-handed player.

Common Faults in Teamwork

1. No agreement as to type of teamwork.
2. Starting and sudden stopping of one player to the confusion of the other.
3. Confusion at net.
4. No agreement as to areas of responsibility for the return immediately following service.
5. Player leaving net immediately after net play.
6. Net player too close to net (in mixed doubles).
7. One player depending too much on partner.
8. One of the partners weak in a particular court.
9. Insufficient use of High Clear.
10. Lack of aggression (i.e., failure to take the offensive often enough).
11. Net player backing up into back player's area.
12. Net player clearing to opposing backcourt player.
13. Failure to take account of partner in the choice of plays.

CHAPTER X

Bird Flight and the Return

In Chapter V, on the subject of bird flight, we listed the *oncoming flight* as a factor in the choice of flight for a return. We shall now consider the return from this standpoint.

In the drawings which follow, oncoming bird flights are illustrated by means of dotted lines and the choice of flight for the return in each case is illustrated by means of solid lines. The choice of return flights are arranged in order of what is generally most effective for the occasion. The choices of return of course represent the ideal situation and may vary with the particular circumstances or according to the "type of game" which the individual plays.

Naturally, the individual's own ability to execute any one of the flights, from his position at the moment, will be a limiting factor. Also, tactics may vary according to the weakness or strength of his opponent in a given situation. The most we can do here is to present the subject in outline, leaving with the reader the responsibility of studying the diagrams in the light of his own experience and expanding them to fit his own game strategy.

As already noted, the Smash is the "kill shot," and the High Clear is the defensive weapon with which the player may gain the necessary time to get out of trouble. The High Clear is also a safety device, being frequently used when the occasion does not present a ready alternative.

In receiving the Short Service, for example, the strongest offense will be a "rush to the net," with a Smash or Drop return. If the opportunity for rushing does not present itself to the alert receiver, it is more than likely due to the fact that the server has kept the flight low and accurate; in this case, an underhand Drop is the logical play for an opening since it draws the receiver to the net and places him on the defensive. The last choice is a High Clear to the weakest backcourt.

To take another example, the Smash (always to be executed from overhead) is again the first choice when receiving the High Clear, provided the oncoming High Clear is short of the backcourt. From the backcourt, the distance is too great for an effective Smash; from the backcourt, therefore, first choice is the overhead Drop. The third and fourth choices (High Clear and Drive) are defensive choices when late for the return, that is, when the bird has fallen too low for the Drop or Smash. The fifth choice, the underhand Drop, is an effective return but difficult for anyone but the expert.

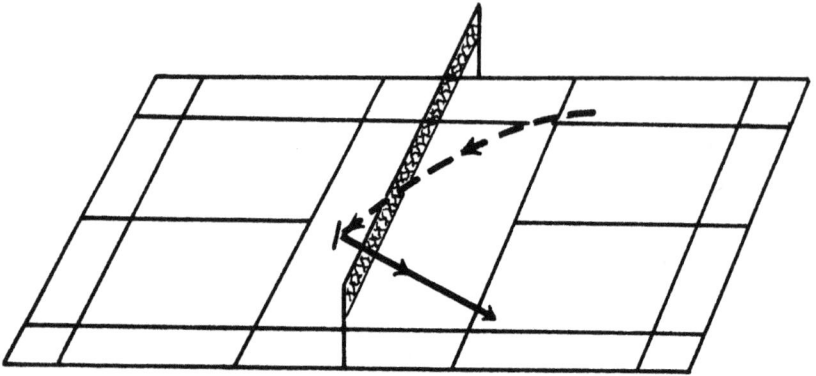

(1) Returning the short service with a smash

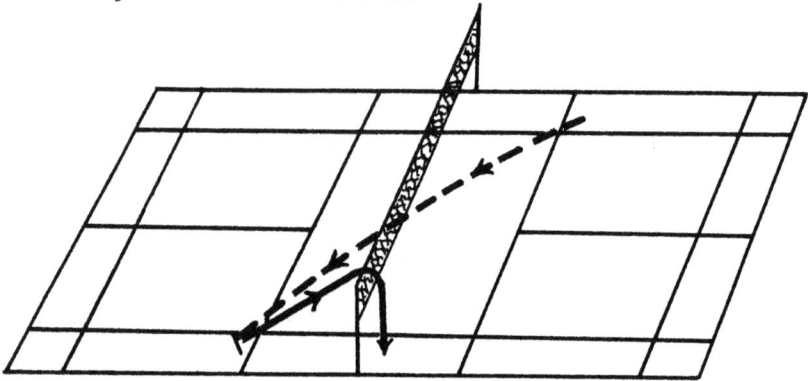

(2) Returning the short service with a drop

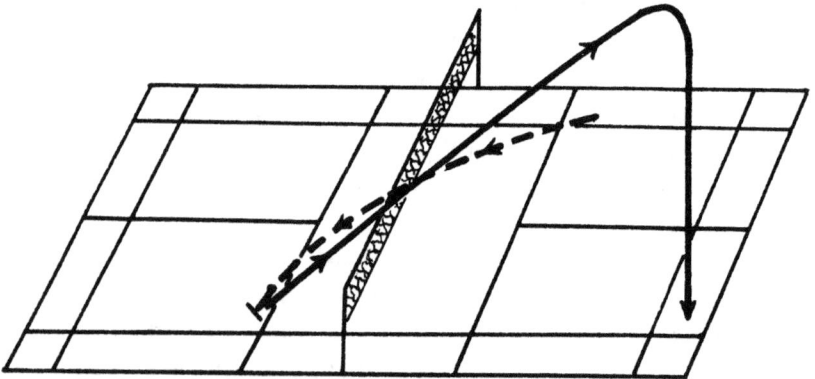

(3) Returning the short service with a high clear

Fig. 27: *Bird Flights and The Return* I. Returning the Short Service.

Choice of Flight: (1) Smash, drop or drive, after "rushing the net." (Offensive) (2) Drop—to weaker alley. (Playing for an opening) (3) High Clear—to weak corner of backcourt.

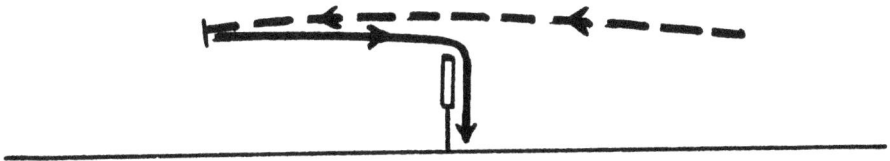

(1) Returning the drive with a drop

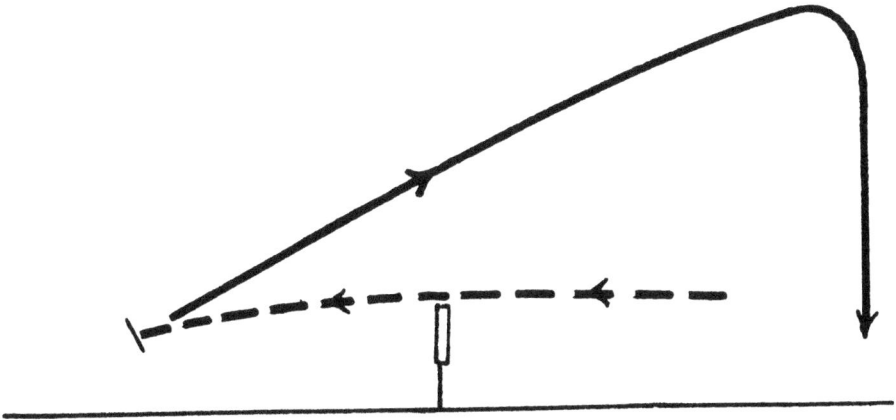

(2) Returning the drive with a high clear

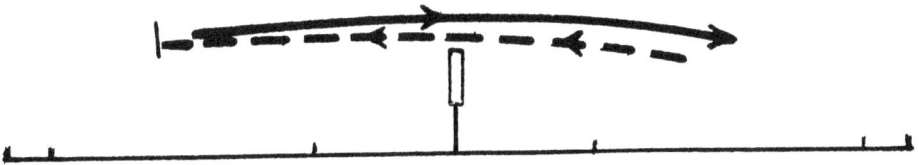

(3) Returning the drive with a drive

Fig. 28: Bird Flights and The Return II. Returning the Drive

Choice of Flight: (1) Drop—to weaker alley. (Playing for an opening) (2) Clear—to weakest backcourt point. (Defensive) (3) Drive—at vulnerable spot. (Defensive but dangerous)

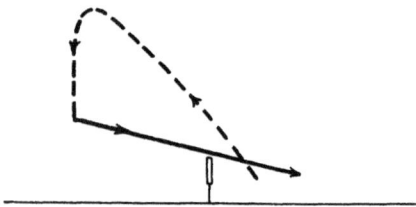

(1) Returning the high clear with a smash

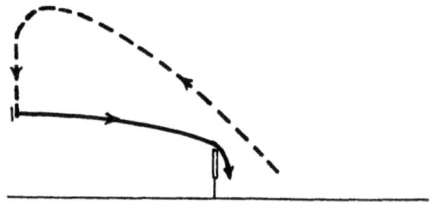

(2) Returning the high clear with a drop

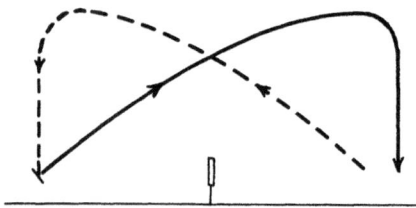

(3) Returning the high clear with a high clear

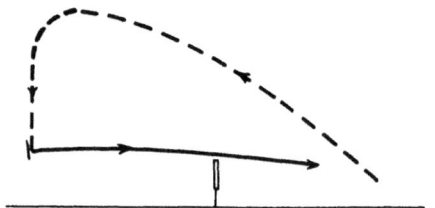

(4) Returning the high clear with a drive

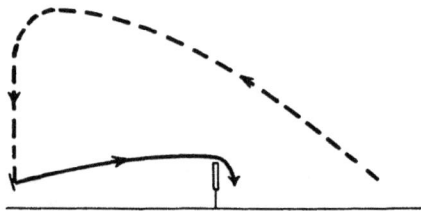

(5) Returning the high clear with a drop

Fig. 29: Bird Flights and The Return
III. Returning the High Clear

Choice of Flight:
(1) Smash—when clear is short. (Offensive)
(2) Drop — to weaker alley (Playing for an opening)
(3) Clear—when in trouble. (Defensive)
(4) Drive — when bird too low for overhead drop. (Defensive, and of doubtful effectiveness.)
(5) Drop—as substitute for drive (if player's proficiency gives him necessary accuracy)

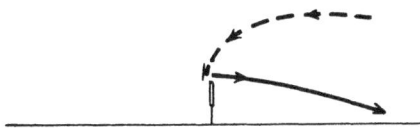

(1a) "Rushing" a drop at the net

(1b) Returning a net flight with a smash

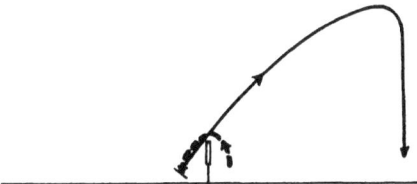

(3) Returning a net flight with a cross-court

(4) Returning a hairpin net flight with a hairpin

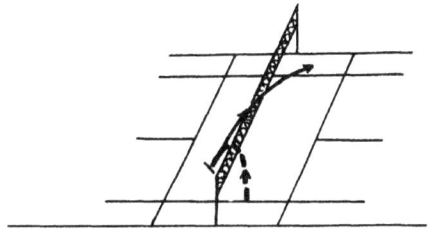

(2) Returning a net flight with a high clear

Fig. 30: Bird Flights and The Return
IV. Returning the Net Flights

Choice of Flight:
(1) Smash, drop, or drive, after "rushing the net." (Offensive)
(2) Clear—when space at net is adequate. (Defensive)
(3) Cross-court—to opposite alley. (Playing for opening)
(4) Hairpin. (Playing for an opening)
(Note: The above applies to returning the drop)

(1) Returning the smash with a drop

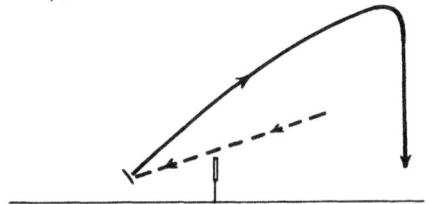

(2) Returning the smash with a high clear

Fig. 31: Bird Flights and The Return
V. Returning the Smash

Choice of Flight:
(1) Drop — to weaker alley. (Playing for an opening)

(2) Clear—to weak backcourt point. (Defensive)

93

CHAPTER XI

Pointers on General Strategy*

Having considered the general factors in the choice of bird flight and the return flights best suited to a given situation, we may now consider the general points of strategy in more detail, and without specific reference to the type of flight which may be involved. With what has been said concerning bird flight, the reader may decide for himself, in any given situation, the type of flight best suited to carrying out any one or combination of the points suggested below. Actual playing situations are of course more or less complicated and diverse; hence the simplification of them is limited. However, we believe that the consideration of bird flight as such, followed with a brief summary of the general points of strategy, will give the reader a background with which he may more readily work out his own strategy in each situation.

In the following outline some repetition occurs, so that it serves not only to amplify but to summarize our previous remarks concerning strategic play. The outline presents a general summary of the *vulnerable situations* which the alert player will be constantly ready to take advantage of. Incidentally, this might also be considered as a list of common playing faults.

Players are frequently caught in one or more of the following *vulnerable situations*:

1. Out of court position (causing a weak court)

   (a) Because of poor footwork

   (b) By failing to return to center of court area after completing a stroke. (See Fig. 19, shaded court areas)

2. Off balance (causing weak court)

   (a) Moving as bird is struck

   (b) Victim of deceptive preliminary stroking

   (c) Not recovered from previous stroke

3. Racket out of stroking position

   (a) Racket not carried in on-guard position. (See Figs. 18 and 24)

   (b) Not recovered from previous stroke. (Example: On racket follow-through in short serve, server is vulnerable to quick placement to forehand)

---

*From: "Journal of Physical Education—Y.M.C.A."—July-August, 1938.

4. Weaknesses of the individual player
   (a) Poor or inaccurate short serve
   (b) Weak backhand
   (c) Poor timing of overhead strokes
   (d) Failure to "rush" high or inaccurate short serve
   (e) Stroking not developed for long flights. (Failure to clear to backcourt)
   (f) Slow in covering court
      1. Poor footwork
      2. Poor balance
   (g) Vulnerable to placements at the body
   (h) Weak at backcourt play
   (i) Easy victim of deception
   (j) Lack of, or inaccurate Smash
   (k) Lack of a 'round-the-head Smash
5. Weaknesses in teamwork
   (a) No agreement as to type of teamwork
   (b) Starting and sudden stopping of one partner to the confusion of the other
   (c) Confusion at net
   (d) No agreement as to areas of responsibility for the return immediately following service
   (e) Player leaving net immediately after net play
   (f) Net player too close to net (in mixed doubles)
   (g) One player depending too much on partner
   (h) One of the partners weak in a particular court
   (i) Insufficient use of High Clear

Besides taking advantage of the above vulnerable situations, the following *offensive tactics* are a part of general strategy:
   (a) Conceal your intentions
   (b) Use stroking deception. (Example: Feint Smash when Dropping; feint Clear on Net play; feint stroking direction)
   (c) Drop (or Clear) on hard Smashes
   (d) Keep flights low so that opponent is forced to stroke upward (playing into your more offensive strokes)
   (e) Make placements to the unobvious spot. (Example: Two consecutive returns to the same court spot will frequently catch opponent out of position as he returns to center of court area)

(f) Direct placements to body at specific points which will prove awkward to the opponent at that moment. (Example: Placement to left shoulder when racket is on the right side)

(g) Place opponent in awkward position at every opportunity

(h) Test your opponent for his stroking repertoire

(i) Cover net on your partner's Smash

(j) Run your opponent—keep him on the move by placing bird out of easy reach (it makes for weak return, opening for next play, and exhausts opponent)

(k) Keep your opponent in the backcourt as much as possible (from there he will be unable to make a severe return)

A *final* word of *warning*:

1. Don't "pop-up." (Keep the bird down.)

2. Don't try to "murder" the bird. (Let the swing of the end of the racket do the work.)

3. Don't make your intentions obvious.

4. Don't let your opponent draw you into his type of game.

5. Don't leave the net immediately after net play. (A net play makes you responsible for the net area on the next return.)

6. Don't start for the bird and then stop, to the confusion of your partner.

7. Don't be "afraid" of a Smash directed to the body. (Your difficulty with this is your fear complex.)

8. Don't stand straight up and flat-footed. (Be "on your toes".)

9. Don't wait until it is time to stroke before you pick out your opponent's point of vulnerability.

10. Don't carry your racket low. (Keep it prepared for quick defense and overhead action.)

11. Don't take your eyes off the bird.

12. Don't change your grip.

CHAPTER XII

The Fundamental Strokes Analyzed

In our early treatment of the fundamental strokes we did not go into a detailed treatment of the wrist-snap and flick. We shall at this point give consideration to this important phase of badminton technique.

The Forehand Stroke

The 1st picture of Figure 32 shows the player in the on-guard position, waiting for the bird to be struck by his opponent. Note his stance and the position of the racket. Both suggest alertness, and preparedness to return the bird from either side or any point. The feet are well apart, the left foot is forward and the left leg is slightly flexed at the knee.

The swing of the racket in the forehand and backhand strokes describes the letter "C" (with a long tail on the end) as it is commonly written in longhand. In the 3rd picture the player has already maneuvered into position to return the bird on his right side. (See: Footwork) Note in the backswing that the wrist leads the racket and that the face of the racket is parallel with the line of movement. This is accomplished by a slight turning of the racket from the wrist.

In the 4th picture the backswing is completed and the downswing has begun. It is important to keep the wrist leading the racket throughout the swing, until a moment before contact. The wrist-lead is shown clearly in the forward swing of the racket (5th picture). At this moment the player is at the point of bringing the racket head forward by means of a quick snap of the wrist.

A moment before contact the wrist is also suddenly withdrawn to produce the flick. That this has been done is clearly shown in the 6th picture. There is a follow-through with the completion of the stroke—this, and the fact that the flick is done so quickly make it practically imperceptible, except in slow-motion pictures (of which these sketches are an exact copy). The flick adds a movement to that of the full sweep of the racket. A very fast flight may be produced only by means of this wrist-snap and flick.

Note that the left foot is well forward and that the bird is permitted to fall to about the knee level. This gives more time for a full-sweeping backswing and makes it unnecessary to hurry the stroke. Note too that the body is bending forward and that the bird is contacted well out in front, both of which permit full freedom of the arm.

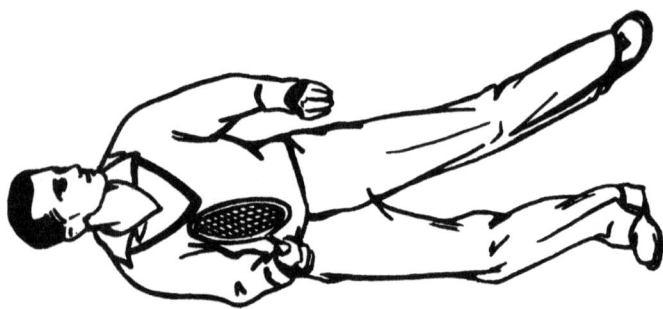

(2)

(1)

Fig. 32: *The Forehand Stroke*

(4)

(3)

Fig. 32 (cont.) : The Forehand Stroke

99

(6)

(5)

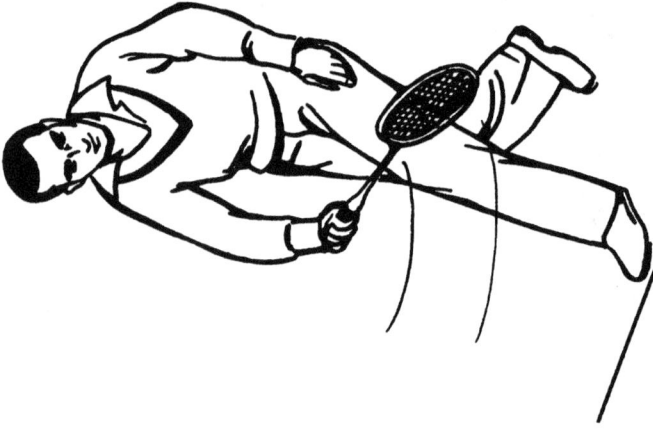

Fig. 32 (cont.) : The Forehand Stroke

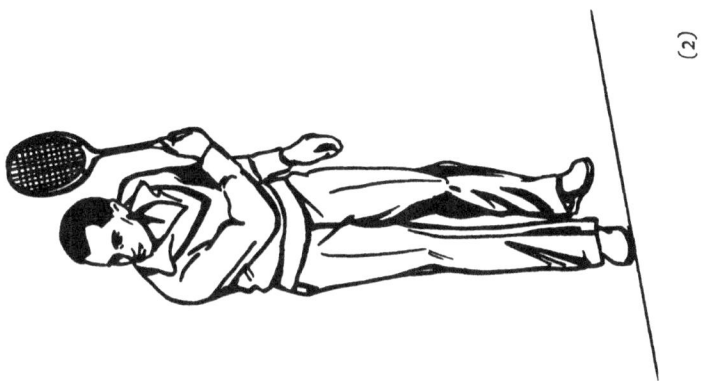

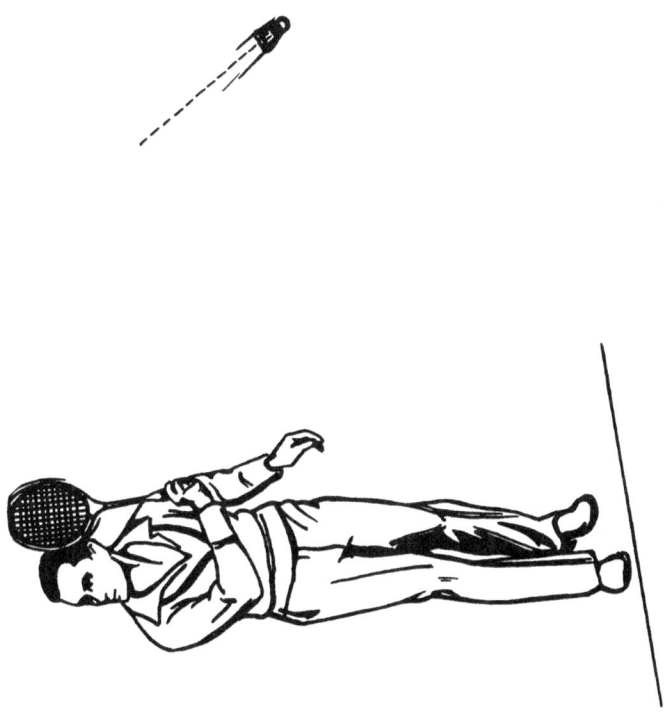

Fig. 33 : *The Backhand Stroke*

(3)

(4)

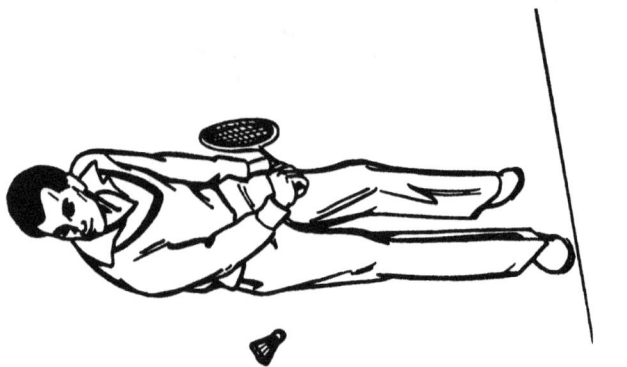

Fig. 33 (cont.) : *The Backhand Stroke*

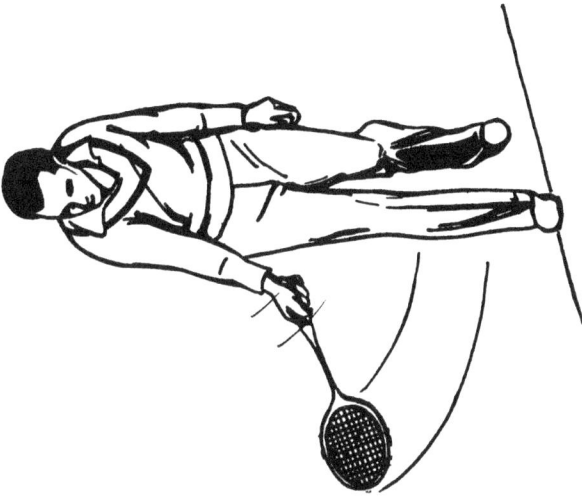

(6)

Fig. 33 (cont.) : *The Backhand Stroke*

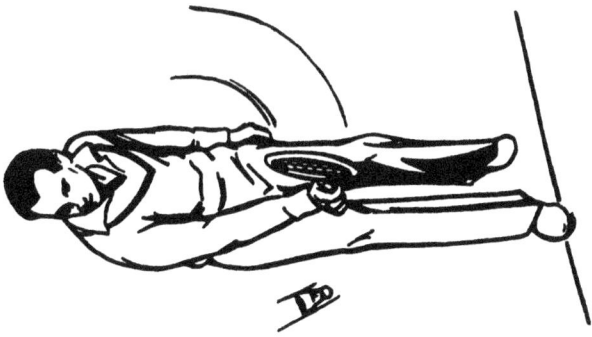

(5)

103

(7)

Fig. 33: (cont.): *The Backhand Stroke*

The Backhand Stroke

In the 1st picture of Figure 33 the player has already maneuvered into position (See: Footwork) and has assumed the stance for a backhand stroke. The right foot is forward this time instead of the left. This permits a turning of the shoulder so as to get a free and full backswing in the stroke. The stroking movement itself is essentially as in the forehand.

The action-strip of the backhand begins (1st picture) with the racket cocked as the backswing begins. In the backswing (2nd picture) the racket is turned from the wrist so that the racket face is parallel with the line of movement and the wrist leads the racket. Note how the face of the racket is turned on the downswing (3rd picture) and how the wrist continues to lead. In the forward part of the stroke (4th picture) the wrist-lead is clearly evident.

In the 5th picture the wrist-snap has begun as the bird is about to be contacted. A moment later and just before the bird is hit the wrist will be quickly withdrawn, giving a whip to the racket which suddenly increases the momentum of the racket head. The action and result here are much the same as in the cracking of a whip. As in the forehand, there is a follow-through which, together with the speed of action, makes the wrist-snap and flick hardly perceptible to the eye.

104

The action-strip of the backhand shows clearly the relative importance of the wrist action as compared to the swing of the arm as a whole. With a wrist action developed as pictured here, a long backward sweep such as is used in the tennis stroke is not necessary. Here the backswing consists largely of a cocking of the racket. The beginner, however, will do well to use a long, sweeping backswing until he has mastered the flick.

As in the forehand, the bird is not struck until it is directly in front of the body and at or near the knee level. This, together with the fact that the player has not maneuvered too close to the bird, permits a full extension of the arm and freedom of action, both necessary to accomplish the wrist action described.

The Overhead Stroke

The overhead stroke is usually executed with all the power at the player's command. Ideally (and when time permits), a full sweep or wind-up of the racket is thus desirable. In the 1st picture of Figure 34, the player has already maneuvered into position for the stroke and has assumed the stroking stance.

In maneuvering into position, it is most important to estimate the proper court spot for the stance since this and the timing of the stroke determine the point at which the bird-racket contact is made. The speed and direction of bird flight resulting from the stroke depend to a considerable extent on this contact point.

The point of bird-racket contact should be a little out in front of the head and line of the body (preferably about 18 inches) and at a full reach of the arm and racket. (See 7th picture.) Maneuvering too close to the bird results in hitting it directly overhead (or back of the head) for a weak Smash or none at all. Hitting the bird too late (down too low) is of course the result of poor timing and affects the stroke likewise.

Note the position of the feet and racket in the 1st picture. The left foot is forward and pointing in line with the oncoming bird. Most of the weight at this moment is on the left foot; the racket has been raised a little from its on-guard position preparatory to beginning the full-sweeping or wind-up movement. Pictures 1 to 5 constitute the wind-up in preparation for the final up-swing of the stroke (6th picture).

In the wind-up, the weight is gradually shifted to the rear (right) foot. On the up-swing (6th picture) the weight is again shifted—to the forward (left) foot—and at the moment of contact all the weight is on the left foot as the player reaches for and strokes the bird with all his might.

Note in the 2nd picture that the racket face is parallel with the line of

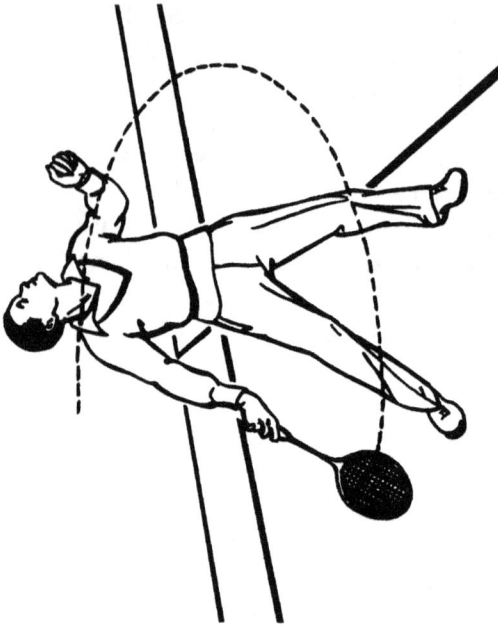

(2)

(1)

Fig. 34: *The Overhead Stroke*

(4)

(3)

Fig. 34 (cont.) : *The Overhead Stroke*

Fig. 34 (cont.) : *The Overhead Stroke*

(8)

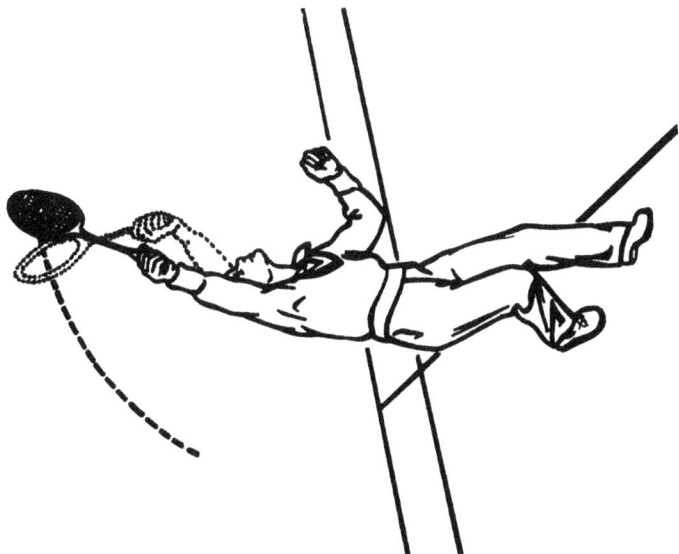

(7)

Fig. 34 (cont.) : *The Overhead Stroke*

movement. At the completion of the backswing in the wind-up (i.e., in the interval between the 2nd and 3rd pictures), the racket is turned from the wrist so that the opposite face is toward the observer. However, the face of the racket continues parallel with the line of movement until an instant before contact, when it is turned from the wrist to meet the bird with the flat face. The bird should not be cut as the ball is in tennis.

At the completion of the wind-up (at a point about midway between the 5th and 6th pictures) the racket is allowed to drop down perpendicularly before the final up-swing of the stroke itself begins. The power is applied to the stroke on the up-swing. Note in the up-swing (6th picture) that the wrist leads the racket (as in the forehand and backhand strokes). This wrist-lead is essential for the "wrist-snap" and "flick" which are shown in the 7th picture.

The wrist-lead is maintained until a moment before contact. Just before contact is made, the racket is brought forward (ahead of the wrist) by means of a quick snap of the wrist. The flick is introduced by a sudden withdrawal of the wrist at the instant of the snap. This sudden flick or withdrawal of the wrist "adds a movement," as it were, to that of the racket swing itself.

CHAPTER XIII

Filling in the Stroking Gaps

The fundamental strokes do not of course provide the player with a complete stroking repertoire. There are certain gaps which call for a modification of the more fundamental forehand, backhand, and overhead strokes. The complete stroking repertoire has been aptly referred to as "stroking by the clock."

For practical purposes, we will have completed the stroking picture with a consideration of the following: (1) The shoulder-high drive, (2) Returning the Smash, (3) The 'round-the-head stroke, and (4) The high backhand.

The Shoulder-High Drive

The shoulder-high drive (Figure 35) serves to meet the situation where the oncoming flight is fast and the bird shoulder-high (too low for a Smash) but not more than a step away. It is very effective for quick placements and finds its use mostly in doubles. Being used for *quick* placements, the time element is all-important. For this reason the ordinary niceties of footwork and windup are not adhered to. The bird is stroked at a full reach of the arm, usually

(1)

Fig. 35a: *The Shoulder-High Drive—Forehand*

112

(3)

(2)

Fig. 35a (cont.): *The Shoulder-High Drive—Forehand*

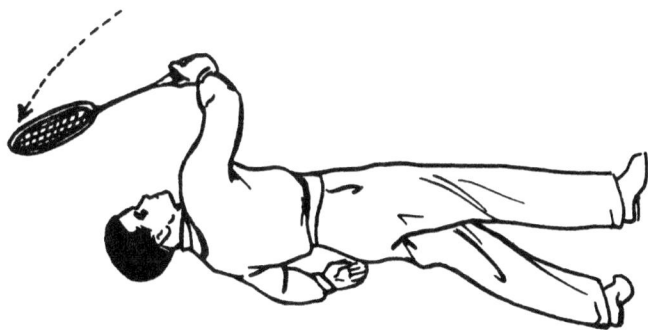

Fig. 35b: *The Shoulder-High Drive—Backhand*

113

with the stroker facing the net rather than attempting to take the orthodox stance for a forehand or backhand. The stroke is a small circular swing with a short windup entirely from the arm and wrist—just enough to get a wrist-snap and flick.

Returning the Smash

We are concerned here more specifically with the Smash (or Drive) directed at the body. There are three vulnerable points in placements at the body: (1) the right hip, (2) the left knee, and (3) the left shoulder.

The first thing required in returning birds directed at the body is to overcome a natural fear which causes one to jerk back. This tendency may be overcome in a very few minutes of practice—by having someone hit hard Smashes or Drives directly at you.

Figure 36a illustrates the returning of a Smash or Drive directed to the right hip or forehand side of the body. To return, keep your eye on the bird; pivot quickly to the right, and allow the bird to go just past the body. Don't stroke the bird—merely let it hit the racket and bound off. The force of the flight is sufficient to send it back over the net. In his excitement, the beginner invariably tries to stroke the bird—and if he is fortunate enough to hit it, the result is usually a pop-up. The main difficulty in returning a Smash directed at the body is in getting the body out of the way.

Figure 36b illustrates the return of a Smash directed to the left knee or backhand side of the body. The principle is much the same as in the forehand return—keep your eye on the bird and let it bound off the racket. Rather than pivot, however, you merely lean or step forward (into the bird). It is not necessary to pivot since the body offers no interference with the arm and racket in this case. For this reason players usually find it easier to return Smashes directed at the body with a backhand, unless of course they are too far over to the right. The same method may be applied to returning a smash in front of the body, by simply bending farther forward.

Figure 36c illustrates the return of a drive or smash directed at the left shoulder. The stroke is a 'round-the-head, which will receive separate and detailed treatment in the following section, since it is applicable to other situations.

Figure 36d illustrates the inferior way to return a Drive or Smash directed at the left shoulder.

'Round-the-Head Stroke

The 'round-the-head stroke is the most effective means of dealing with

114

(a) Forehand

(b) Backhand

(c) 'Round the head

(d) Weak return

Fig. 36: *Returning the Smash*

115

(2)

(1)

Fig. 37 : *The 'round-the-head Stroke*

(4)

(3)

Fig. 37 (cont.) : The 'round-the-head Stroke

117

(5)

Fig. 37 (cont.) : *The 'round-the-head Stroke*

flights directed to the left side of the head or the left shoulder. For this reason it is an effective means of returning a Driven Serve to the backhand corner. (See discussion of Placement Points in Chapter VIII.) It may also be used in returning high flights to the extreme left hand corner of the backcourt, provided the player is fast enough to get into position before the bird falls too low.

More power and deception are possible in this stroke than in a high backhand. Also, it leaves the player in a better position for the next play. In receiving the serve it permits the receiver to stand closer to the net (for rushing) since he will still be in position to return a Driven Serve to the backhand corner. One may Smash, Clear, or Drop with the stroke. As in the case of the overhead, a Drop is made more effective by feinting a Smash or using cross-court deception. Flights as low as the elbow level may be dealt with by quickly dropping from the knees.

The 1st picture of Figure 37 shows the racket in the early part of the backswing. It is being swung out, away from the head and shoulders, so as to get a full circular swing around the head. At the early part of this backswing, the racket is turned from the wrist so that the face of the racket is parallel with the line of the backswing movement.

The 2nd and 3rd pictures show the racket in the circular swing around

118

Fig. 38: *The High Backhand Stroke*

the head; the 4th picture shows the contact, as the circular swing around the head nears completion. A wrist-lead is maintained throughout the swing, until a moment before contact, as in the forehand, backhand, and overhead strokes. This of course makes a wrist-snap and flick possible.

Well planned and carefully executed footwork is essential for this stroke. When standing still, the right or left-foot-forward stance may be used. However, when moving, only the left-foot-forward stance, as in the overhead stroke, should be used. The left foot in this case should be pointed approximately towards the center of the opponent's court—this places the body and shoulders in position to contact the bird at the angle required to direct it within the court boundary. The weight is shifted backward by bending from the hips and knees. This gives a wide sweep to the racket and maximum power.

The High Backhand Stroke

The high backhand is not a very offensive stroke, being practically limited to the Drop and High Clear flights. In the preceding section we pointed out that a 'round-the-head stroke is preferable to the high backhand, if there is time for getting into position, since it is more offensive and leaves the player in a

119

better position for the next play. However, the high backhand is a very useful and at times indispensable stroke. In fact, in some sections, the 'round-the-head stroke is not taught at all, there being a strong preference for the high backhand.

The stroke may be best made with a full extension of the arm and a thumb-up grip. (See Figure 38) Pointing the right foot toward the backcourt and turning the back to the net permits a full backswing, which is essential when clearing with this stroke. The stroke itself otherwise involves the same principles as the low backhand.

CHAPTER XIV

Selection and Care of Equipment

If he shops around, the beginner in any sport is usually confronted with a bewildering variety (in makes, styles, and prices) of equipment. A few guiding principles will, however, enable him to make a wise choice of a badminton racket without personal assistance.

A common error is to select cheap equipment at the start, on the assumption that it is "good enough" until one attains some proficiency in the game. The beginner's performance is affected by the type of equipment he uses just as much as the advanced player's, if not more. Moreover, a better grade of equipment is cheaper in the long run.

The price of a good badminton racket, based on cost, will usually be evenly distributed between the frame and the string.* A good frame, properly cared for, will last a long time and take many re-strings. Fifty per cent of the investment in a quality racket is therefore more or less permanent. Thus with the stringing impaired half of the cost still remains in salvage value; its resale value is for this reason largely in the frame. A good frame moreover will take a tight stringing, which is not the case with an inferior one. A tight stringing is essential for distance of flight and responds better to the fine touch so often necessary in badminton play.

Selecting a Racket**

Aside from quality, there are five points to consider in selecting a racket: weight, balance, stringing, grip, and flexibility of shaft. The beginner should use a racket with an overall weight of less than five ounces. It is well to remember that ⅛ of an ounce makes a great deal of difference in the weight of a racket. The 4 to 5 ounce indoor racket should not be used for standard outdoor play where a weighted or rubber-tipped bird is used.

---

*Rackets range in price from three to fifteen dollars. A recent Y.M.C.A. survey, made under the direction of Harold L. Kistler of Newark, N. J., and discussed at the 1938 International "Y" Championships in Detroit, showed that 45% of the purchases made by the "Y" players covered in the survey were in the four to five dollar price range, and that 25% were above this. Our experience and inquiry among players indicate that the purchasers will do best in the price range beginning at five dollars. A standard brand of a recognized manufacturer is further recommended.

**The section of this chapter dealing with selection and care of rackets appeared in "The Sporting Goods Dealer"—August, 1938.

Balance is important in that it determines the weight of the head as compared to the rest of the racket. A "heavy-headed" racket is harder to wield than a "light-headed" one. This is particularly true for the beginner whose nerve reaction time tends to be slower than that of the experienced player. Besides being clumsy and a tax on the beginner's strength, it interferes with the wrist-snap and flick which he will eventually develop. Also, the lighter head is better suited to the finesse required to produce the Net and Drop flights. With the heavy-headed racket, on the other hand, a more severe smash may be executed. For the beginner, however, the argument is strongly in favor of the lighter head.

The balance of the racket (including the gut) may be determined by tying a string around the shaft, shifting the racket until it hangs balanced, and then measuring the distance from the balancing point to the tip of the handle. If this distance is within the range of 11¼ to 11¾ inches the racket may be said to be well-balanced. (A balance at 11½ inches is probably the ideal.) When the distance from the tip of the handle to the balancing point is greater than 11¾ inches, the head is definitely on the heavy side.

For all-around purposes, 20 gauge, clear gut is the most satisfactory. Clear gut is generally more durable than the colored variety. A little lighter gut (21 gauge) is sometimes preferred for tournament play since it may be strung a little tighter without too much strain on the frame.

We have already mentioned the importance of a tight string. We indicated too that the rigidity of the frame sets a limit on the tightness which it may safely carry. However, a racket can be strung too tightly regardless of the rigidity or strength of the frame. In that case the strings themselves become hard and inflexible. The tightness of string may be determined by placing the end of the handle against the face bone just under the ear and gently brushing the strings with the backs of the finger tips, that is, with the finger nails and in a direction away from the racket handle. A tone comparable to C sharp at middle C (on the piano) indicates a satisfactory tightness; that comparable to D or D sharp is well suited to most players.

The racket handle should be octagonal in shape (not round or oval), and with the facets of varying widths. The two facets parallel to the face of the racket should be larger than the others. These are the facets which lay against the palm of the hand and the tip of the thumb. The two facets in line with the side of the racket head should be slightly narrower and the four remaining ones smaller than this again. This shape of handle helps prevent the racket from slipping and enables the player to *feel* whether or not his grip is correct.

The handle should not be larger than the player may firmly grip though the size is fairly well standardized and as such suited to most players. In general, some type of leather or fabric is desirable as a covering. Leather, perforated with small holes, is a common and fairly satisfactory covering. Some attempts are being made to develop a "sweat-proof" and "slip-proof" composition; the results may have some merit.

The racket shaft should have some flexibility but it may easily have too much. The flexibility may be tested by taking hold of the handle with one hand and the tip with the other and trying to bend the shaft. There should be some bend without having to apply much force, but it should not bend so easily as to have too much "whip" in it. A shaft with too much "whip" will definitely interfere with the accuracy and effectiveness of the player's strokes.

Care of the Racket

A racket press and a rubberized, waterproof cover should be purchased along with the racket. Temperature and humidity affect the frame and strings of a racket tremendously and will quickly damage them if reasonable precautions are not taken. Being of lighter construction than the rackets used in other games, that used in badminton is more quickly affected by changes of temperature and humidity. The tighter the string, the more easily the frame tends to warp. Once warped, a frame is permanently misshaped.

The press and racket cover minimize the effects of temperature and humidity changes. These safeguards together with a few simple precautions will insure a maximum of good service without much trouble. The racket should be hung up by means of a string tied to the handle. It should never be stood on end for any length of time. If placed in the press so that the tip does not protrude beyond the edge of the press, there is less likely to be any damage done if the racket is accidentally dropped. The racket should not be stored in the basement or attic. Extremes of heat in the one case hasten the deterioration of the strings, and dampness in the other tends to warp the frame and rot the strings. The usual first floor is the best place for storage.

Very rarely, if ever, are rackets broken by sheer power of stroking. Practically without exception they are broken as a result of hitting the floor, another racket or some other object—this in turn is usually the result of carelessness. Care should be taken not to scrape rough floors when picking up the bird. Remember that the strings protrude to some extent despite the precaution of countersinking them in the head. Incidentally, the countersinking has a tendency to weaken the frame slightly.

Selection and Care of Birds

Shuttlecocks are made from imported goose feathers, the finest cork, kid and linen binding. Domestic feathers are not suitable. The method of weighting involves specialized machinery and processes.

Birds are graded at the factory according to color, size, and durability of the feather shafts. The better shafts are larger (hence tougher) and more uniform in size, quality, and color.

There is a great deal of variation in the practices employed by the various manufacturers in making birds. These differences are noticeable in the gluing, binding at the base and mid-point of the feather, etc. It is well to consider these factors when selecting birds for season's play. Constant changing from one make of bird to another is not a wise practice since each make has certain definite characteristics which call for slight variations in play when a change is made.

The birds indicated as "Fast" on the container are sometimes erroneously thought of as superior to a slower or medium-fast type of bird. It is well to remember that the faster the bird, the more difficult the play and probably the less enjoyable the game for the average player. When lighting conditions are not ideal, a slower bird will increase the fun of the game since there will be less misses and strike-outs due to the lighting factor. Extremely fast birds change the game to such an extent that the player hardly recognizes his own game. The same is also true of an extremely slow bird. (For flight characteristics as prescribed by the Rules, see Appendix B, Laws of Badminton—Rule No. 4.)

Unskilled players injure birds more rapidly than players who hit accurately and squarely. Every attempt, therefore, should be made to hit the bird with the face of the racket. Flipping it with the racket from the floor to the server, and sending it along the floor, are very injurious. If it cannot be picked up with the racket, without injury, pick it up and throw it to the server. This practice will greatly increase the life of the bird.

Before serving, make it a practice to straighten the feathers. The shafts may be straightened and the feathers put back into place quickly and easily. This not only preserves the bird but makes for a truer flight.

The most important single factor in determining the life of a bird is the place of storage. Birds are sensitive to changes of temperature—which in turn affects their durability and flight. When allowed to become dry, the feather shafts become brittle and break off easily. Birds should be kept in a cool, damp place such as a refrigerator (if properly humidified), a fruit cellar, or garage floor. A temperature of around 60 deg. F. and a relative humidity ranging from 70 to 80 are the most satisfactory.

Some players dampen the feathers before playing to decrease their brittleness and prolong their life. This treatment, however, is not advisable and is entirely unnecessary if the birds are stored properly.

A factor in this connection is the temperature and humidity of the gym or hall itself. If the room is warm and the air dry, the birds will of course dry out quickly no matter how carefully they were cared for before play. Room temperature of course affects the speed of the game also. Blowing the breath into the space between the feathers during play helps to keep them from drying out.

Glossary of Terms

Alley—(side alley)—The narrow strip (1½ feet wide) between the two side boundary lines. (See Fig. 7)

Anchor fingers—The little finger and the two adjoining ones. These fingers (when holding the racket) keep the handle in place; the index finger and thumb serve more to direct the movement of the racket. (See Fig. 1)

Anticipation—Foreseeing or forejudging opponent's intended play.

Back boundary line—There are two back boundary lines, 2½ feet apart. The outer line is the back boundary of the playing court for both singles and doubles. It is also the long service (or back boundary) line of the singles service court. The inner line serves as the long service (or back boundary) line of the doubles service court only. (See Fig. 7)

Backcourt (back alley)—Area between the two back boundary lines, and immediately in front of this. (See Fig. 7)

Backhand stroke—Stroke used in returning a bird from the left side of the body. In the forward part of backhand, the *back* of the hand is, of course, in front of the racket handle. (See Figs. 12, 13, 33, 35 and 36)

Balance (of body)—Body position permitting easy movement in the desired direction.

Balance (of racket)—Distribution of weight throughout the racket.

Bird—See shuttlecock.

Bird flight—Path of bird's flight after it is hit. (See: Drive, High Clear, Driven Clear, Drop, Smash, Short Serve; Long, High Serve; Driven Serve, Net flights.)

Court spot—Any small area on the court, selected for placement of the bird or for the stroking stance.

Cross-court (net) flight—A flight in which the bird is directed along and close to the net-tape, falling in or near the alley. (See Figs. 9 and 30)

Dead bird—See: Out of play.

Deception—Disguising one's intentions to lead opponent to anticipate the play wrongly, as in feinting stroke, flight or placement.

Diagonal teamwork—Division of responsibility according to a line drawn from the back right-hand corner of the court to the intersection of the side boundary line and the net (left side). One player assumes responsibility for the front triangle, the other for the back triangle. (See Fig. 26)

Doubles—The four-handed game.

Doubles service court—(also referred to as right or left half-court)—Area between the midcourt (center) line and the outer side boundary line, and between the short service line and the inner back boundary line. (See Fig. 7)

Down—Loss of serve occasioned by the server's (or serving side's) failure to score. In doubles, each side has two downs (except in the first inning of the game), that is, each of the partners has a turn at serving before relinquishing the serve to the opposing side. In the first inning, the side first serving has only one down.

Drive (or driven flight)—A fast flight, parallel or nearly so to the floor. (See Figs. 9, 28 and 29)

Driven clear—A flight directed over opponent's head and out of his immediate reach, toward the backcourt, but with less height than the High Clear. (See Fig. 9)

Driven serve—Refers to flight of serve which is long but low in contrast to the Long, High Serve; used mostly in doubles.

Drop—A rapidly descending flight, directed close to the net. May be an underhand or overhead Drop. (See Figs. 9, 27, 28, 29 and 31)

Face of racket—The oval, stringed area.

Facet—One of the sides of the racket handle. The handle of a badminton racket is ordinarily octagonal, with two wide facets (parallel with the stringed area) and three narrower facets between these and on either side.

Fault—"Fault" is used here in two slightly different ways—one in connection with technique and the other in connection with the Laws of Badminton. A "fault," as used in the Laws of Badminton, is an infraction of the rules resulting in forfeiture of the serve if committed by the server (or serving side) or in a point gained for the serving side if committed by the player or side *not* serving. (See Appendix B—Laws of Badminton—Faults) "Fault" as used in connection with technique carries its usual meaning—in this case, incorrect or poor technique, with no penalty attached other than less effective play.

Fingering the grip—Moving the index finger or thumb slightly forward on the racket handle to assist in directing the stroke. The index finger is moved forward for the forehand, the thumb for the backhand. This does not alter the grip. (See Figs. 11 and 13)

Flexible wrist—Wrist position which permits full freedom of wrist. In the lower forehand and backhand strokes, the racket and hand holding it should be tilted up slightly to permit full flexibility of the wrist. (See Fig. 1)

Flick—Sudden withdrawal of the wrist near the completion of a stroke and just before the bird is contacted. The action is similar to that in cracking a whip; the result is that the head of the racket or tip of the whip is brought forward with greatly accelerated speed. The flick occurs immediately after the wrist-snap. In a sense, the flick is a part of the wrist-snap, being a completion of the entire wrist action. We prefer, however, to consider them as separate since this gives a clearer picture of what actually happens. (See Figs. 23 and 34)

Flight—See: Bird flight.

Footwork—Action of the feet in maneuvering to the bird and in recovering court position. Also, position of feet in stroking. (See Fig. 19)

Forehand stroke—Stroke used in returning a bird from the right side of the body. In the forward part of the forehand, the racket handle is, of course, directed by the *fore* part of the hand. (See Figs. 10, 11, 32, 35 and 36)

Game—The regular game constitutes 15 points in doubles and men's singles, and 11 points in women's singles.

Game bird—The service which, if resulting in or followed by a point for the server, wins the game. When the server has 14 points, for example, and he needs but one point to win the game, the bird is said to be a "game bird" as it is served.

Grip—The racket hold. (See Fig. 1)

Hairpin (net) flight—A short flight made from close to the net. Ideally, the bird should cross close to the net-tape and fall close to the other side of the net. (See Figs. 9 and 30)

Half-court (right or left)—See: Doubles service court, Singles service court.

Hand out—See: Down.

High clear—A rapidly ascending flight, the bird being directed high overhead and falling in the backcourt. (See Figs. 9, 27, 28, 29, 30 and 31)

Home position—Ideal spot on the court where player awaits return of opponent. This is a spot from which access may be most easily gained to all parts of the court area for which the player is responsible. After the return, the player proceeds to this spot if possible. (See Fig. 19)

In (service)—Player or side serving.

Inning—A side's turn at serving.

In play—The bird is "in play" from the time it is hit by the server and until it hits the floor or the body or clothes of any player, or until a "fault" is committed. See: Out of play. (See: Appendix B—Laws of Badminton)

Kill return (or shot)—The shot or placement that makes a return impossible under the circumstances.

Let—Permitting the serve to be made over, occasioned by: the bird being served so that it hits the net-tape but falls within the proper service court; an unforeseen or accidental hindrance coming in the way of a player.

Lift stroke—A stroke used in returning the bird from close to and directly over the net. "Lift" describes the racket movement. It is not meant to imply that the bird itself is lifted over the net. It is, rather, gently but distinctly hit, resulting in what is to a considerable extent a bounce of the bird from the racket. (See Fig. 16)

Lob—See: High clear, Driven clear.

Locked (or humped) wrist—Inflexible wrist resulting from racket handle being held parallel with the forearm or pointed down. (See Fig. 2)

Long, high serve—Refers to flight of serve which is long and high (High Clear), directed to the backcourt; used more in singles than in doubles. (See Fig. 20)

Long serve—A serve directed to the backcourt. See: Long, high serve; Driven serve.

Long service line—See: Back boundary line.

Midcourt (or center) line—Extends from short service line to back boundary line, dividing this area into two equal portions; serves as inside boundary line dividing the service courts. (See Fig. 7)

Net flights—See: Hairpin flight, Cross-court flight.

Net play (or strokes)—See: Lift stroke, Rushing, Cross-court and "hairpin" flights.

Net-tape—White cotton binding tape along the top of the net.

On-guard stance—Alert position assumed by a player when waiting for the bird to be hit by opponent. (See Fig. 18)

Out (of service)—Player or side receiving the service.

Out-of-hand serve—A serve executed by hitting the bird out of the hand; suited to producing the Short and Driven Service flights only. (See Fig. 5)

Out of play—A bird is out of play when it hits the floor, body or clothes of the player, or a "fault" is committed by a player. (See Appendix B—Laws of Badminton)

Overhead stroke—Stroke used in returning a bird from an overhead point. Ideally, a stance should be assumed and the stroke timed so as to contact the bird a little out in front, *not* directly overhead. (See Figs. 14 and 34)

Pivot—Turning the body on the ball or toe of the foot. The other foot serves to "push off" but the movement is actually begun and directed by the head and shoulders.

Placement—Direction of the bird to a specific spot on the court or at the opponent.

Placement points (in the serve)—Specific spots on the receiving court at which the serve is aimed and directed. (See Fig. 20)

Play for an opening—Maneuvering opponent into position for the "kill."

Playing court—Court area when the bird is in play, that is, following the service. Comprises the area between the net and the outer back boundary line (for singles and doubles), and between the side boundary lines (the inside lines in singles and the outside lines in doubles). (See Fig. 7)

Point of bird-racket contact—Any aerial point at which the bird is struck by the racket.

Pop-up—A slow, high flight, the bird falling short or close to the net. Pop-ups are the result of a faulty technique; they are the perfect "set-up" for a smash or other "kill" return.

Rotation teamwork—A side-by-side formation with the players rotating sides according to prearrangement and when strategically advantageous to do so. (See Fig. 26)

'Round-the-Head stroke—Stroke used in returning overhead or shoulder-high flights on the left side of the body. This is a circular, 'round-the-head movement in which the racket is turned so as to stroke the bird forehanded. It is a modification of the overhead stroke, and avoids the weaker high backhand return. (See Figs. 36 and 37)

Rubber—The best of 3 games in regulation matches.

Rushing—Rushing to the net and returning the bird with a short, quick overhead stroke (or modification of this). Rushing is confined to the player close enough to the net to reach the pop-ups and slow flights which clear the net-tape by too wide a margin. (See Fig. 15)

Service (or serve)—Act of placing the bird into play at the start of a regular game. The service is classified here in two different ways: according to the type of delivery of bird to racket (out-of-hand, toss), and according to the type of flight involved (Short; Long, High; Driven). (See Figs. 5, 20 and 23)

Set—See: Setting.

Setting—Increasing game points when the score is tied at 2 or 1 less than game points. In a 15-point game, when the game is tied at 13, it may be set 5 points; when tied at 14, it may be set 3 points. In an 11-point game, when tied at 9, it may be set 3 points; when tied at 10, it may be set 2 points. The option of setting rests with the player or side first reaching the tied score.

Set-up—Popping up or otherwise placing oneself open for a "kill" return from opponent.

Short serve (sometimes called "soft serve")—Refers to flight of serve which is short, i.e., just over the short service line; most commonly used in doubles. (See Figs. 9 and 20)

Short service line—Front boundary line of service court, parallel with and 6½ feet from the net. (See Fig. 7)

Shoulder-high drive—A forehand or backhand stroke used in making a quick return of a bird at shoulder height and within reach without moving from the spot. (See Fig. 35)

Shuttlecock—Frequently called shuttle or bird. "Bird" is generally favored in the United States for its brevity. For description and specifications of the regulation bird, see Appendix B, Laws of Badminton, paragraph 4.

For further description and pointers on selection and care of birds, see Chapter XIV.

Side-by-Side teamwork (sometimes called "sides")—Division of responsibility roughly corresponding to an equal division of the playing court. The dividing line is the midcourt line, extended to the net. (See Fig. 26)

Side boundary line—There are two side boundary lines, 1½ feet apart. The outer line is the side boundary of the doubles playing and service court. The inner line is the side boundary of the singles playing and service court. (See Fig. 7)

Sides—See: Side-by-Side teamwork.

Singles—The two-handed game.

Singles service court (also referred to as right or left half-court)—Area between the midcourt (center) line and the inner side boundary line, and between the short service line and the outer back boundary line. (See Fig. 7)

Sling—See: Throw.

Smash—A rapidly descending flight, very fast and at sharp angle to the floor. (See Figs. 9, 27, 29, 30, 31 and 36)

Stance—Position of feet and body while waiting for the bird and while stroking. (For service stances, see Figs. 3, 21, 23 and 24. For on-guard stance, see Fig. 18. For stroking stances, see Figs. 10, 12 and 14)

Teamwork—Prearranged agreement as to areas and situations for which each of the teamed players is responsible. There are four well known fundamental systems: side-by-side, up-and-back, diagonal, and rotation.

Throw—(or sling)—An indistinct hit or sliding contact between the racket and bird, usually the result of catching the feathers in the strings or of drawing the racket away from the bird as it is stroked. This constitutes a "fault" according to the rules.

Thought action—Action prompted by step-by-step thinking ahead of the play rather than by mere impulse or chance.

Toss serve—A serve executed by means of tossing the bird out in front (and to the side) of the body. Suited to producing any of the service flights— Short; Driven; or Long, High. (See Fig. 23)

Trim—String at both ends of the racket face, looped over the lengthwise strings. The side showing the loops is called the "rough" side.

Up-and-Back teamwork—Division of responsibility according to a lateral division of the court. In general, the "up" player assumes responsibility for the net area (between the short service line and the net) ; the "back" player assumes responsibility for the remainder of the court; used in mixed doubles. (See Fig. 26)

Volley—Exchange of the bird following the serve.

Vulnerable situation—Situation of weakness in which the player or team is open to attack.

Wrist-snap—Use of the wrist to bring the racket head forward. The wrist-snap and flick may be used in all strokes: forehand, backhand, overhead, and long, high serve. In order to "snap" the wrist, it is essential that the wrist *lead* the racket in the forward swing of the stroke. A sweeping stroke with ample backswing is necessary but this, without the wrist-snap and flick, is not sufficient to give much force to an object as light as the badminton bird. (See Figs. 23, 32 and 33)

The Laws of Badminton

As revised in the year 1939 and adopted by
the International Badminton Federation

Copyright, 1939, American Badminton Association
Reprinted by permission of the American Badminton Association

1. (a) COURT—The court shall be laid out as in Diagram "A" (except in the case provided for in paragraph "b" of this Law) and to the measurements there shown, and shall be defined by white, black or other easily distinguishable lines, $1\frac{1}{2}$ inches wide.

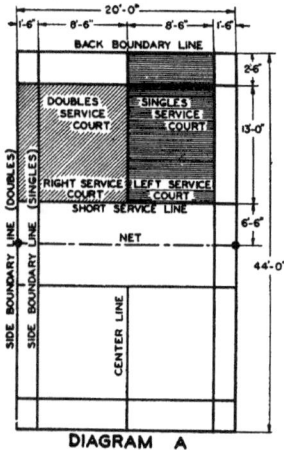

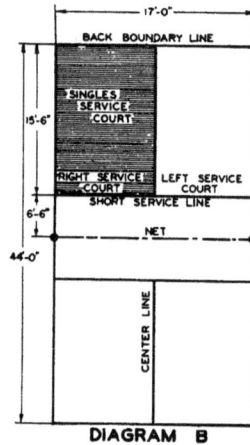

DIAGRAM A   DIAGRAM B

In marking the court, the width ($1\frac{1}{2}$ inches) of the center lines shall be equally divided between the right and left service-courts; the width ($1\frac{1}{2}$ inches each) of the short service line and the long service line shall fall within the 13 foot measurement given as the length of the service-court; and the width ($1\frac{1}{2}$ inches each) of all other boundary lines shall fall within the measurements given.

(b) Where space does not permit of the marking out of a court for doubles, a court may be marked out for singles only as shown in Diagram "B." The back boundary lines become also the long service lines, and the posts, or the strips of material representing them as referred to in Law 2, shall be placed on the side lines.

2. POSTS—The posts shall be 5 feet 1 inch in height from the floor.

134

They shall be sufficiently firm to keep the net strained as provided in Law 3, and shall be placed on the side boundary lines of the court. Where this is not practicable, some method must be employed for indicating the position of the side boundary line where it passes under the net, e.g., by the use of a thin post or strip of material, not less than 1½ inches in width, fixed to the side boundary line and rising vertically to the net cord. Where this is in use on a court marked for doubles it shall be placed on the side boundary line of the doubles court irrespective of whether singles or doubles are being played.

3. NET—The net shall be made of fine tanned cord of ¾ inch mesh. It shall be firmly stretched from post to post, and shall be 2 feet 6 inches in depth. The top of the net shall be 5 feet in height from the floor at the center, and 5 feet 1 inch at the posts, and shall be edged with a 3 inch white tape doubled and supported by a cord or cable run through the tape and strained over and flush with the top of the posts.

4. SHUTTLE—A shuttle shall weigh from 73 to 85 grains, and shall have from 14 to 16 feathers fixed in a cork, 1 inch to 1⅛ inches in diameter. The feathers shall be from 2½ to 2¾ inches in length from the tip to the top of the cork base. They shall have from 2⅛ to 2½ inches spread at the top and shall be firmly fastened with thread or other suitable material.

In places where atmospheric conditions, due either to altitude or climate, make the standard shuttle unsuitable the specifications in this Law may be modified subject to the approval of the National Organization concerned.

A shuttle shall be deemed to be of correct pace if, when a player of average strength strikes it with a full underhand stroke from a spot immediately above one back boundary line in a line parallel to the side lines, and at an upward angle, it falls not less than 1 foot, and not more than 2 feet 6 inches, short of the other back boundary line.

5. (a) PLAYERS—The word "Player" applies to all those taking part in a game.

(b) The game shall be played, in the case of the doubles game, by two players a side, and in the case of the singles game, by one player a side.

(c) The side for the time being having the right to serve shall be called the "In" side, and the opposing side shall be called the "Out" side.

6. TOSS—Before commencing play the opposing sides shall toss, and the side winning the toss shall have the option of:—

(a) Serving first; or (b) Not serving first; (c) Choosing Ends.

The side losing the toss shall then have choice of any alternative remaining.

7. (a) SCORING—The doubles and men's singles game consists of 15 or 21 points, as may be arranged. Provided that in a game of 15 points, when the score is 13 all, the side which first reached 13 has the option of "setting" the game to 5, and that when the score is 14 all, the side which first reached 14 has the option of "setting" the game to 3. After the game has been "set" the score is called "love all," and the side which first scores 5 or 3 points, according as the game has been "set" at 13 or 14 all, wins the game. In either case the claim to "set" the game must be made before the next service is delivered after the score has reached 13 all or 14 all. Provided also that in a game of 21 points the same method of scoring be adopted, substituting 19 and 20 for 13 and 14.

(b) The ladies' single game consists of 11 points. Provided that when the score is "9 all" the player who first reached 9 has the option of "setting" the game to 3, and when the score is "10 all" the player who first reached 10 has the option of "setting" the game to 2.

(c) A side rejecting the option of "setting" at the first opportunity shall not be thereby debarred from "setting" if a second opportunity arises.

(d) In handicap games "setting" is not permitted.

8. The opposing sides shall contest the best of 3 games, unless otherwise agreed. The players shall change ends at the commencement of the second game and also of the third game (if any). In the third game the players shall change ends when the leading score reaches:—

(a)   8 in a game of 15 points;

(b)   6 in a game of 11 points;

(c)   11 in a game of 21 points;

or, in handicap events, when one of the sides has scored half the total number of points required to win the game (the next highest number being taken in case of fractions). When it has been agreed to play only one game the players shall change ends as provided above for the third game.

If, inadvertently, the players omit to change ends as provided in this Law at the score indicated, the ends shall be changed immediately the mistake is discovered, and the existing score shall stand.

9. (a) DOUBLES PLAY—It having been decided which side is to have the first service, the player in the right-hand service-court of that side commences the game by serving to the player in the service-court diagonally opposite. If the latter player returns the shuttle before it touches the ground, it is to be returned by one of the "in" side, and then returned by one of the "out" side, and so on, till a fault is made or the shuttle ceases to be "in play" (see paragraph (b)). If a fault is made by the "in" side, the servers' hand is

136

out, and as the side beginning a game has only one hand in its first innings (see Law 11), the player of the opposing side in the right-hand service-court now becomes the server; but if the service is not returned, or the fault is made by the "out" side, the "in" side scores a point. The "in" side players then change from one service-court to the other, the service now being from the left-hand service-court to the player in the service-court diagonally opposite. So long as a side remains "in," service is delivered alternately from each service-court into the one diagonally opposite, the change being made by the "in" side when, and only when, a point is added to its score.

(b) The first service of a side in each inning shall be made from the right-hand service-court. A "Service" is delivered as soon as the shuttle is struck by the server's racket. The shuttle is thereafter "in play" until it touches the ground, or until a fault or "let" occurs. After the service is delivered, the server and the player served to may take up any positions they choose on their side of the net, irrespective of any boundary lines.

10. The player served to may alone receive the service, but should the shuttle touch, or be struck by, his partner the "In" side scores a point. No player may receive two consecutive services in the same game.

11. The side beginning a game has only one hand in its first innings. In all subsequent innings each partner on each side has a hand, the partners serving consecutively. The side winning a game shall always serve first in the next game, but either of the winners may serve and either of the losers may receive the service.

12. If a player serves out of turn, or from the wrong service-court (owing to a mistake as to the service-court from which service is at the time being in order), *and his side wins the rally*, it shall be a "Let", provided that such "Let" be claimed or allowed before the next succeeding service is delivered.

If a player standing in the wrong service-court takes the service, *and his side wins the rally*, it shall be a "Let", provided that such "Let" be claimed or allowed before the next succeeding service is delivered.

Should a player inadvertently change sides when he should not do so, and the mistake not be discovered until after the next succeeding service has been delivered, the mistake shall stand, and a "Let" cannot be claimed or allowed.

13. SINGLES PLAY—In singles Laws 9 to 12 hold good except that:—

(a) The players shall serve from and receive service in their respective right-hand service-courts only when the server's score is 0, or when he has scored an even number of points in the game, the service being delivered from and received in their respective left-hand service-courts when the server has scored an odd number of points.

(b) Both players shall change service-courts after each point has been scored.

14. FAULTS—A fault made by a player of the side which is "in", puts the server out; if made by a player whose side is "out", it counts a point to the "In" side.

It is a fault:—

(a) If in serving, the shuttle at the instant of being struck be higher than the server's waist, or if any part of the head of the racket, at the instant of striking the shuttle, be higher than any part of the server's hand holding the racket.

(b) If, in serving, the shuttle falls into the wrong service-court (i.e., into the one not diagonally opposite to the server), or falls short of the short service line, or beyond the long service line, or outside the side boundary lines of the service-court into which service is in order.

(c) If the server's feet are not in the service-court from which service is at the time being in order, or if the feet of the player receiving the service are not in the service-court diagonally opposite until the service is delivered. (See Law 16.)

(d) If before or during the delivery of the service any player makes preliminary feints or otherwise intentionally balks his opponent.

(e) If, either in service or play, the shuttle falls outside the boundaries of the court, or passes through or under the net, or fails to pass the net, or touches the roof or side walls, or the person or dress of a player. (A shuttle falling on a line shall be deemed to have fallen in the court or service-court of which such line is a boundary.)

(f) If the shuttle "in play" be struck before it crosses to the striker's side of the net. (The striker, may, however, follow the shuttle over the net with his racket in the course of his stroke.)

(g) If, when the shuttle is "in play", a player touches the net or its supports with racket, person or dress.

(h) If the shuttle be hit twice in succession by the same player, or be hit by a player and his partner successively, or if the shuttle be not distinctly hit. (See Interpretation 2.)

(i) If in play a player strikes the shuttle (unless he thereby makes a good return), or is struck by it, whether he is standing within or outside the boundaries of the court.

(j) If a player obstructs an opponent.

(k) If Law 16 be transgressed.

15. GENERAL—The server may not serve till his opponent is ready, but the opponent shall be deemed to be ready if a return of the service be attempted.

16. The server and the player served to must stand within the limits of their respective service-courts (as bounded by the short and long service, the central, and side lines), and some part of both feet of these players must remain in contact with the ground in a stationary position until the service is delivered. A foot on or touching a line in the case of either the server or the receiver shall be held to be outside his service-court. (See Law 14 (c).) The respective partners may take up any position, provided they do not unsight or otherwise obstruct an opponent.

17. If, in service, the shuttle touches the net it is a "Let", provided the service be otherwise good. If in the course of a rally the shuttle touches and passes over the net it does not invalidate the stroke. It is a good return if the shuttle having passed outside either post drop on or within the boundary lines of the opposite court. A "Let" may be given by the umpire for any unforeseen or accidental hindrance.

If, in service, the shuttle strikes the top of the net, and is then struck or touched by the player served to, it is assumed that the shuttle would have fallen into the proper service-court, and it is a "Let".

If, in service, or during a rally, a shuttle, *after passing over the net*, is caught in or on the net, it is a "Let." When a "Let" occurs, the play since the last service shall not count and the player who served shall serve again.

18. If the server, in attempting to serve, misses the shuttle, it is not a fault; but if the shuttle be touched by the market, a service is thereby delivered.

19. If, when in play, the shuttle strikes the net and remains suspended there, or strikes the net and falls towards the ground on the striker's side of the net, or hits the ground outside the court and an opponent then touches the net or shuttle with his racket or person, there is no penalty, as the shuttle is not *then* in play.

20. If a player has a chance of striking the shuttle in a downward direction when quite near the net, his opponent must not put up his racket near the net on the chance of the shuttle rebounding from it. This is obstruction within the meaning of Law 14 (j).

A player may, however, hold up his racket to protect his face from being hit if he does not thereby balk his opponent.

21. It shall be the duty of the umpire to call "fault" or "let" should

either occur, without appeal being made by the players, and to give his decision on any appeal regarding a point in dispute, if made before the next service; and also to appoint linesmen at his discretion. An umpire's decision shall be final, but he shall uphold the decision of a linesman. Where, however, a referee is appointed, an appeal shall lie to him from the decision of an umpire on question of law only.

Interpretations

1. Any movement or action by the server that has the effect of breaking the continuity of service after the server and receiver have taken their positions to serve and to receive the service is a preliminary feint.

(See Law 14(d))

2. It is a fault under Law 14 (h) :—

(a) If the shuttle be held on the racket during the execution of a stroke, i.e., if it be caught and slung instead of being distinctly hit, or

(b) If the shuttle be hit twice during the execution of a stroke. But it is *not* a fault (provided the stroke be otherwise legitimate) :

(c) If the base and feathers of the shuttle be struck simultaneously.

(d) If the shuttle be struck by any part of the frame of the racket.

3. It is obstruction if a player invade an opponent's court with racket or person in any degree except as permitted in Law 14 (f).

(See Law 14(j))

4. Where necessary on account of the structure of a building, the local Badminton Authority may, subject to the right of veto of its National Organization, make by-laws dealing with cases in which a shuttle touches an obstruction.

Hints to Tournament Committees

1. All courts at tournaments should be marked out for both singles and doubles play, except where space does not permit of this being done in the case of a court used for singles only.

2. The draw shall be conducted as follows:—Each competitor's name, or the names of each pair of competitors in a doubles event, shall be allotted a number. As many numbers as there are playing units shall be written or printed on separate pieces of card or paper, and placed in a bowl or hat, drawn out one by one at random, and copied on a list in the order in which they have been drawn.

3. When the number of playing units is 4, 8, 16, 32, 64, or any higher power of 2, they shall meet in pairs in the order drawn, as in the following diagram:

1st Round	2nd Round	3rd Round	Final Round

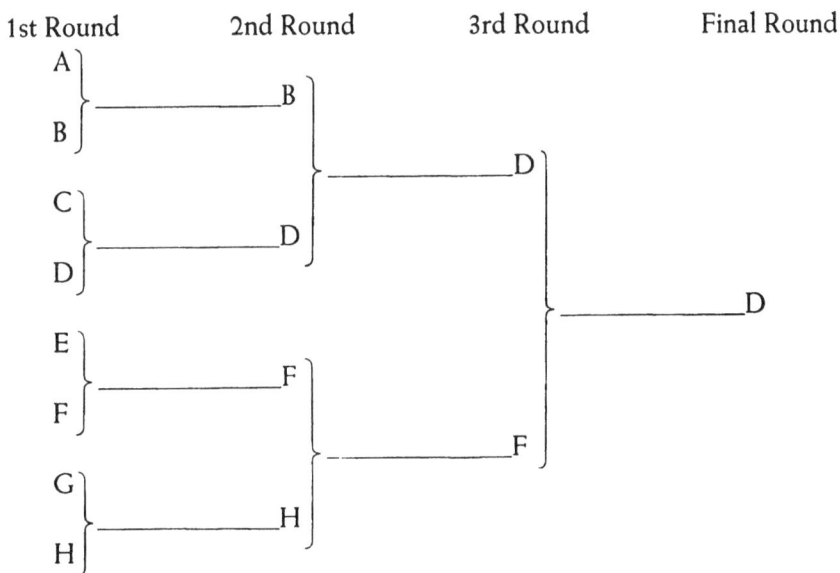

4. When the number of playing units is *not* a power of 2, there shall be byes in the *first* round. The number of byes shall be equal to the difference between the next highest power of 2 and the number of playing units. The byes, if even in number, shall be divided, as the names are drawn in equal proportions at the top and bottom of the list, above and below the pairs; if uneven in number, there shall be one more bye at the bottom than at the top.

141

Example—With 19 playing units there will be $32 - 19 = 13$ byes, 6 at the top and 7 at the bottom of the list, and 3 matches in the first round, 8 in the second, and 4 in the third, etc.

Example—With 9 playing units there will be $16 - 9 = 7$ byes, 3 at the top and 4 at the bottom, and one match in the first round, thus:

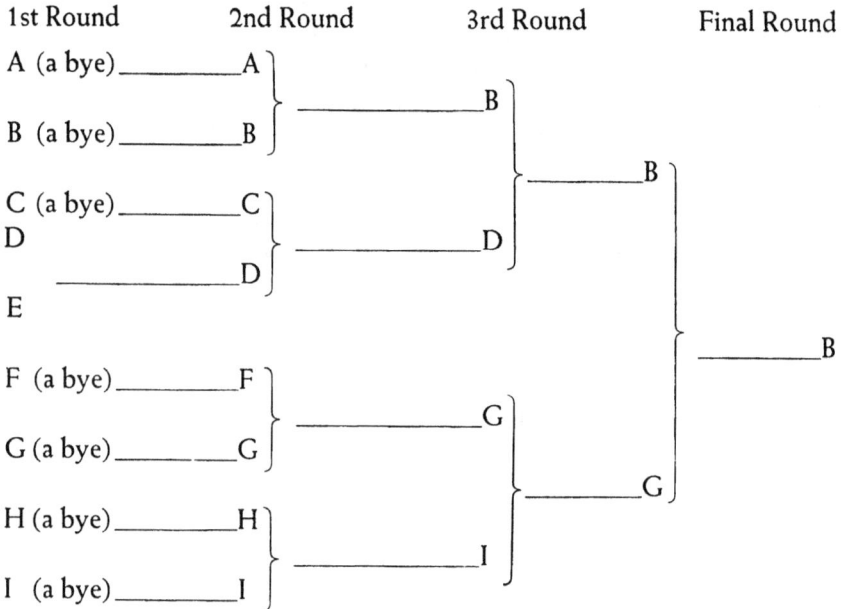

1st Round	2nd Round	3rd Round	Final Round

A (a bye) _____ A ⎫
                    ⎬ _____ B ⎫
B (a bye) _____ B ⎭   ⎬ _____ B ⎫
                               ⎬   ⎬
C (a bye) _____ C ⎫   ⎬ _____ D ⎭
D   ⎬ _____ D ⎭
     _____ D ⎭   ⎬ _____ B
E   ⎬
                                               ⎬
F (a bye) _____ F ⎫   ⎬
                    ⎬ _____ G ⎫
G (a bye) _____ G ⎭   ⎬ _____ G ⎫
                               ⎬   ⎬
H (a bye) _____ H ⎫   ⎬ _____ I ⎭
                    ⎬ _____ I ⎭
I (a bye) _____ I ⎭

With 5 playing units there will be 1 bye at the top and 2 byes at the bottom, thus:

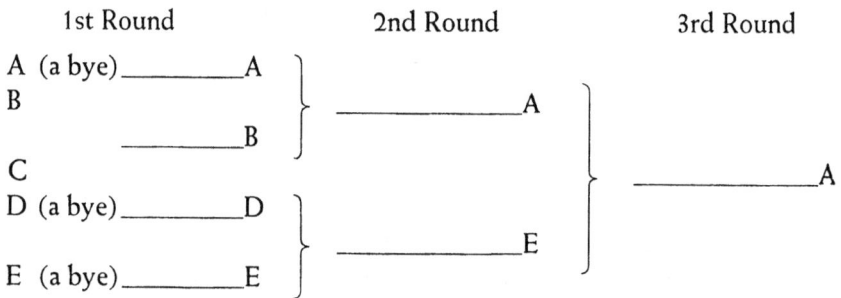

1st Round	2nd Round	3rd Round

A (a bye) _____ A ⎫
B   ⎬ _____ A ⎫
     _____ B ⎭   ⎬ _____ A
C   ⎬
D (a bye) _____ D ⎫   ⎬
                    ⎬ _____ E ⎭
E (a bye) _____ E ⎭

With 6, 1 bye at the top, and 1 bye at the bottom.
With 7, 1 bye at the bottom.
With 8, no byes.
With 9, 3 byes at the top, and 4 byes at the bottom.

142

With 10, 3 byes at the top, and 3 byes at the bottom.
With 11, 2 byes at the top, and 3 byes at the bottom.
With 12, 2 byes at the top, and 2 byes at the bottom.
With 13, 1 bye at the top, and 2 byes at the bottom.
With 14, 1 bye at the top, and 1 bye at the bottom.
With 15, 1 bye at the bottom.
With 16, no byes.
And so on with larger numbers in like manner.

Duties of Umpires

Before Play Commences

1. See that the net is the correct height and satisfactorily fastened to the posts at both top and bottom.

2. See that a supply of tested shuttles is on hand and, during a game, if a change of shuttle is requested the umpire's decision shall be final.

3. If possible see that spectators are not located behind the ends of the court unless some distance away.

4. If there are linesmen see that they understand their duties and their line assignment and request that they call their decisions clearly and promptly.

5. Supervise the toss for choice of service or ends.

6. Introduce the players—when defending champions are competing (in the finals) introduce them first and announce the server.

7. Have a score card ready with names of players on it.

During Play

1. Keep continually on the alert for:

   a. Possible "high" service fault.

   b. Let.

   c. The fall of the shuttle if it be not taken.

   d. That both server and receiver are in their respective court sections at the time of contact of shuttle and racket during service and that some part of both feet of server and receiver are on the floor at the time of contact. If considered necessary the umpire may request a service fault judge at any time.

143

e. Faults.

   During doubles contests exercise great care in recording the number of "hands" in. After each rally announce the score and the number of "hands" in.

3. When a score at which setting is permissible is reached, ask the player who first reached that score whether he or she wishes to set.

4. See that the players change sides at the proper score in the third game and that the ruling regarding rest periods is carried out.

5. Be convinced of a fault before penalizing the striker—if there is any doubt allow the play to proceed without interruption. Faults must be called immediately.

6. Give decisions promptly and loudly enough to be heard by spectators as well as players.

7. If the umpire is unable to give a decision during play, the opinion of the players may be accepted if mutually agreed, otherwise a let shall be declared.

8. The linesman's decision regarding the fall of the shuttle is final—the umpire is not privileged to question it.

9. On the conclusion of the match, announce the winners and scores and present the records of the contest to the referee at once.

Bibliography

Books (and Pamphlets) on Technique

Devlin, J. F.—BADMINTON FOR ALL (Hutchinson & Co., Ltd.—London. American Edition—Doubleday Doran, 1937).

> 128 pages, 17 illustrations.
>
> HOW TO PLAY BADMINTON (Slazengers Canada Limited — Toronto).
>
> Pamphlet—Contains Laws.
>
> 40 pages, 8 illustrations, 2 diagrams.

Ferrers-Nicholson, Mrs. N., and Sid G. Hedges—THE ART OF BADMINTON (Methuen & Co., Ltd.—London, 1934).

> Contains Laws.
>
> 99 pages, 2 diagrams.

Ketchum, Leon—BADMINTON (Chicago Park District, 1937).

> Pamphlet—Contains Laws.
>
> 76 pages, 23 motion picture series, 7 diagrams.

Thomas, Sir George, Bart.—THE ART OF BADMINTON (Hutchinson & Co., Ltd.—London, 1932).

> 156 pages, 16 illustrations.
>
> BADMINTON (Seeley, Service & Co., Ltd.—London, 1936).
>
> Contains Laws.
>
> 52 pages, 7 illustrations.

Tragett, Mrs. R. C.—BADMINTON FOR BEGINNERS (Chatto & Windus—London, 1935).

> 117 pages, 8 illustrations.

Triscott, C. Pette—THE A.B.C. OF BADMINTON (Athletic Publications, Ltd.,—London).

> Pamphlet—Contains Laws.
>
> 59 pages, 8 illustrations.

Uber, E. and H. S.—BADMINTON (Eyre & Spottiswoode, Ltd.—London, 1936).

> Contains Laws.
>
> 119 pages, 6 motion picture series.

Magazines

CANADIAN LAWN TENNIS AND NORTH AMERICAN BADMINTON
—The only magazine on this side of the Atlantic which devotes practically its entire issues (in season) to the sport. Contains articles and news of interest to players in the United States as well as Canada. Published in Montreal, Canada.

SCHOLASTIC COACH—The following articles by Carl H. Jackson and Lester A. Swan may be of interest:

Badminton Mixed Doubles Play (Mar. 1939)

Badminton—The Regular Doubles Game (Apr. 1939)

In Badminton It's the Flick (Dec. 1939, Jan. 1940)

Badminton's Deceptive Plays and Strokes (Nov. and Dec. 1940)

INDEX

INDEX (Continued)

COACHWHIP PUBLICATIONS

COACHWHIPBOOKS.COM

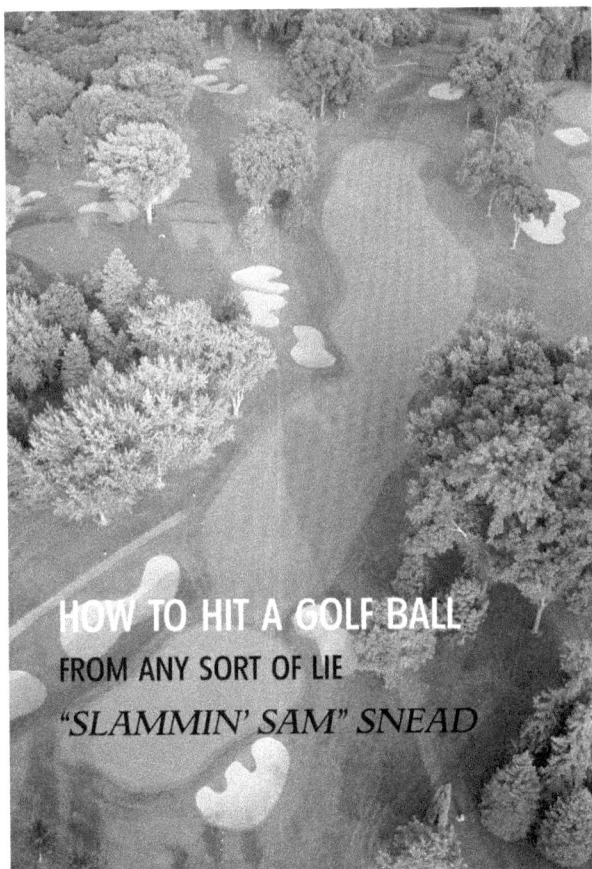

How to Hit a Golf Ball
ISBN 1-61646-203-5

COACHWHIP PUBLICATIONS

COACHWHIPBOOKS.COM

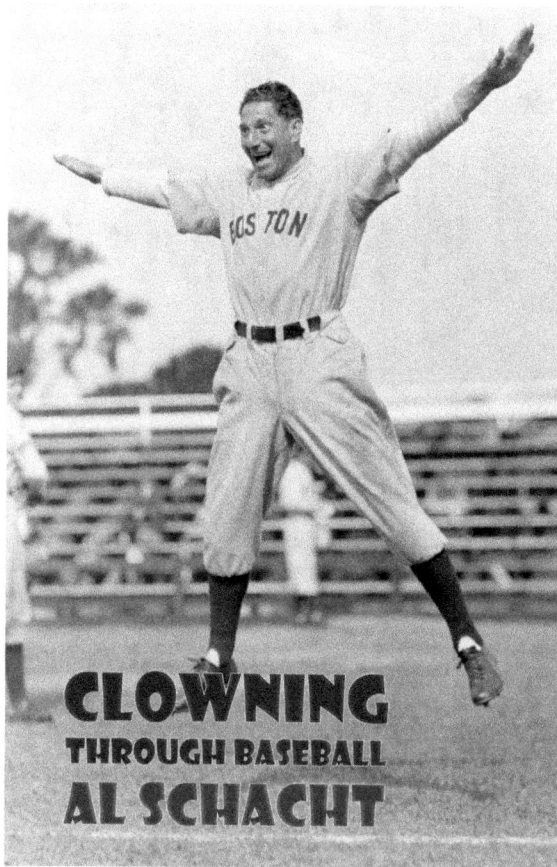

Clowning Through Baseball
ISBN 1-61646-208-6

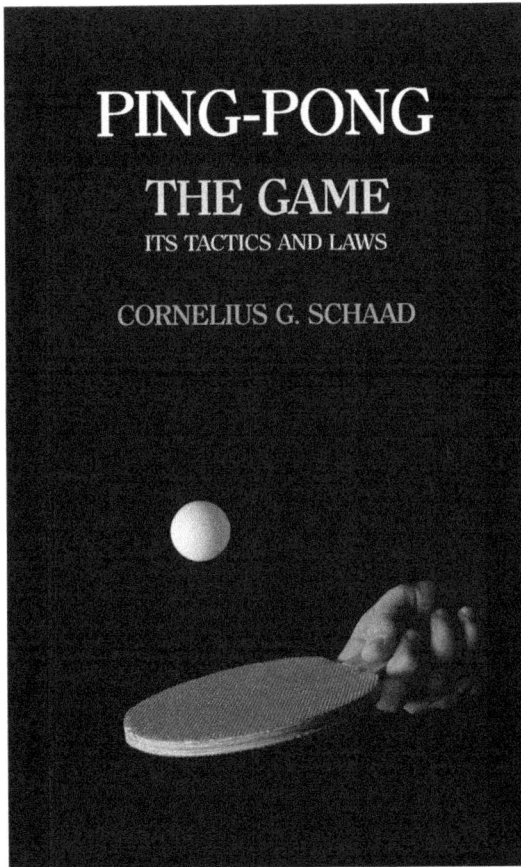

PING-PONG

THE GAME

ITS TACTICS AND LAWS

CORNELIUS G. SCHAAD

Ping-Pong
ISBN 1-61646-224-8

COACHWHIP PUBLICATIONS

COACHWHIPBOOKS.COM

CROQUET

Rules and Strategy for Home Play

PAUL BROWN

Croquet
ISBN 1-61646-144-6

PITCHING
HORSESHOES

Pitching Horseshoes
ISBN 1-61646-204-3